ALABASTER

ntroduction

ıe Bible presents a rich and foundational narrative. Its verses, an-
:nt yet eternally relevant, guide us through the complexities of exis-
ıce, sharing the stories of those who have come before us and illuminating our paths with meaningful truths and timeless lessons. Across cultures and generations, these texts have endured and continue to serve as catalysts for profound wisdom and shared understanding.

And yet, amidst the busy and frenetic pace of modern life, it can be daunting to study scripture. It can be difficult to know where to begin or how to establish a regular rhythm of reading and reflection. Certain passages may intimidate us, requiring historical context to be fully understood. Others present a picture of God we may find challenging, with wrathful language that can strike us as unsettling. How do we find the beauty of the Bible amidst these obstacles?

This study endeavors to provide a guide for spending a year in the Bible. With suggested readings for each day of the week, spanning the various biblical literary genres, we embark on a journey of curiosity and contemplation, exploring the relevance of these ancient words in our contemporary lives. By the end, we will have read through and explored the entirety of the Bible together.

Reading, in this context, is not a passive exercise; it is an active engagement with the sacred. With an overarching reading to help guide our study and thoughtful prompts to invite deeper reflection, this book invites us to explore the story of scripture with fresh eyes and focused intention:

I. Begin each week with a carefully chosen passage from the **READING LIST**, the orienting **SYNOPSIS**, and its accompanying devotional **READING**. This reading serves as our shared compass, spotlighting an overarching theme to accompany our reflections throughout that week.

II. After our foundational readings, we invite you to **REFLECT** on the provided prompts and the accompanying **PRAYER**. These elements act as gateways to deeper introspection. Throughout the week, find moments to revisit and let these words enhance your contemplation.

III. Continue throughout the week to seek moments of quiet and engage with each daily reading through the lens of the week's theme, prompts, and prayers. Through consistent engagement, the timeless truths of scripture resonate more deeply within our daily lives.

As we delve into the intricate narrative of the Bible, let there be joy —a joy born from understanding and insight. In the quiet moments of reflection, may we find not only knowledge but also the wisdom that enriches our lives and the lives of those around us. Amen.

Table of Contents

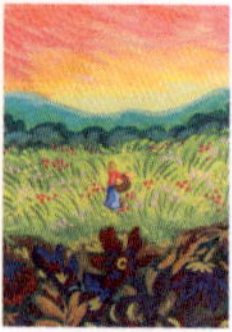

1
Relationship Between God & Humanity
Genesis 1–3

2
Divine Guidance & Provision
Isaiah 7–11

3
New Beginnings
Romans 5–6

4
God's Unbreakable Promises
Genesis 12–15

5
Trust in God's Unfathomable Nature
Psalms 12–14

6
Seeking Inner Righteousness
Matthew 14–16

7
God Delivers Us
Psalms 18–20

8
Heeding God's Calling
Isaiah 40–44

9
Wrestling with Faith & Judgment
Genesis 32–35

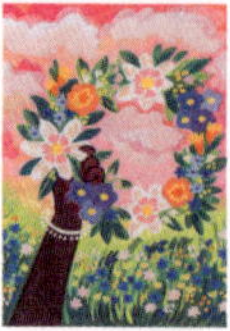

10
Complexity of Relationships
Matthew 26–28

11
Steadfast Faith in Times of Sorrow
1 Samuel 1–5

12
Anticipating a Better Future
Isaiah 62–66

13
Learning from Past Lessons
1 Corinthians 9–10

Weeks 1–26

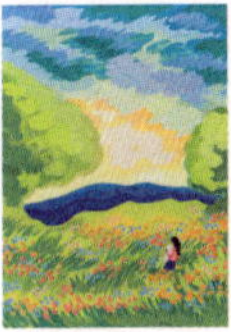

14
God Values the Weak & Vulnerable
Exodus 1–4

15
The Beauty of Serving Others
Mark 9–10

16
God is Our Refuge
Psalms 45–47

17
God is Mighty
Exodus 13–16

18
Hope & Patient Expectation
Jeremiah 27–31

19
God's Vision & Plans
Luke 1–2

20
Living Generously
2 Corinthians 9–10

21
God's Transformative Grace
2 Samuel 20–24

22
Pursuing Wisdom
Proverbs 1

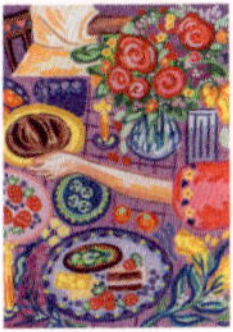

23
Extending Hospitality
Luke 9–10

24
Unity Through Inclusion
Ephesians 1–3

25
Repairing Relationships
Leviticus 4–6

26
Finding God in Quietness
1 Kings 19–22

Table of Contents

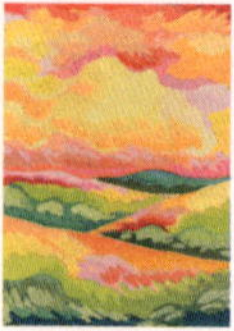

27
The Nature of God's Kingdom
Luke 17–18

28
Freedom & Reconciliation in Christ
Colossians 1–2

29
Divine Justice in an Unjust World
Ezekiel 31–36

30
Community of Believers
1 Thessalonians 1–3

31
Flourishing in God's Presence
Ezekiel 43–48

32
Strength & Perseverance
2 Thessalonians

33
The Joy of Worship
Psalms 96–98

34
The Gift of Forgiveness
John 7–9

35
Divine Callings
1 Chronicles 15–19

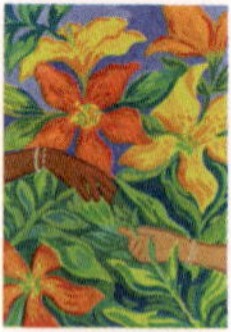

36
The Holy Spirit is Our Advocate
Joel

37
Leading Well
Titus

38
Work of the Cross
John 19–21

39
The Greatness of God
Psalms 114–116

Weeks 27–52

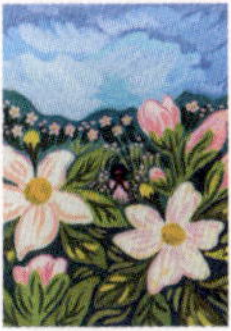

40
Compassion & Second Chances
Jonah

41
Jesus is Our Redeemer
Hebrews 8–10

42
Sharing Our Faith
Acts 7–8

43
Living Out Our Faith
Deuteronomy 4–6

44
Embracing Life's Seasons
Ecclesiastes 3–4

45
Obedience Despite Uncertainty
Deuteronomy 10–12

46
Courage in the Face of Opposition
Acts 15–16

47
God's Enduring Love
Psalms 134–136

48
The Call to Return to God
Malachi

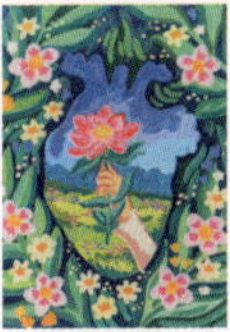

49
The Greatest Commandment (Love)
1 John 4–5

50
The Beauty of Intimacy
The Song of Songs 3–4

51
The Power of Advocacy
Esther 1–5

52
Creation Made Whole
Revelation 18–22

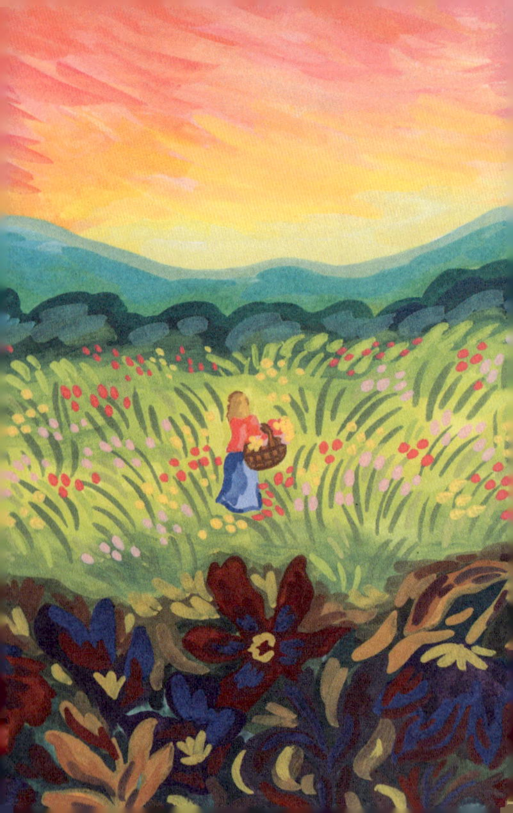

Relationship Between God & Humanity

Synopsis

Humanity shares a unique bond with God, characterized by deep personal intimacy and the invitation to foster a beautiful world. Genesis 1–3 highlights this relationship and sets the stage for the broader biblical story to unfold.

Reading Plan

- ○ Day 1 / Genesis 1–3
- ○ Day 2 / Romans 1–2
- ○ Day 3 / Joshua 1–5
- ○ Day 4 / Psalms 1–2
- ○ Day 5 / Job 1–2
- ○ Day 6 / Isaiah 1–6
- ○ Day 7 / Matthew 1–2

Read—Genesis 1-3

The opening chapters of Genesis paint a vivid picture of a world teeming with life. In this intricate ecosystem, every element, from the largest creatures to the smallest plants, is interconnected, contributing to the overall beauty and health of the garden. It is good. The interrelatedness of the world highlights the inherently relational nature of our Creator's design. And, as we see in Genesis, no relationship is more central to the story of scripture than that of the profound bond between God and humanity.

Significantly, from the very first days of Eden, the Creator isn't merely observing. This isn't a distant deity, aloof and passive. Rather, God intimately communes with Adam and Eve. God breathes life into humanity, signifying not just an igniting spark of existence, but also the onset of a deeply personal relationship. Being crafted in God's image isn't about mere appearance; it denotes a shared spirit, a mutual essence between Creator and creation. Eden's serene moments perfectly encapsulate this, as daily walks and earnest conversations with God showcase a bond of deep camaraderie.[1] This connection is reinforced in God's assurance in Joshua 1:9—"Do not be afraid; do not be discouraged, for the Lord your God will be with you wherever you go."

The nature of humanity's relationship with God stands apart from that of the rest of creation. We aren't merely inhabitants of this evolving terrain but its designated stewards. Humanity is empowered not with unchecked authority, but a deep-seated duty. Our role? To protect every tree and every creature, ensuring all thrive under our care. In this way, we mirror the care, grace, and compassion that God extends to us.

As numerous passages throughout scripture show us, we are hardly perfect in this role. We see early errors in Genesis 3 devolve into a verifiable pattern of mistakes, as outlined in Isaiah 1 and Romans 1. And yet, God persists in pursuing us, continually drawing us back to the beauty and harmony etched into the fabric of creation.

As we immerse ourselves in these biblical passages this week, may we consider these aspects of our relationship with God. Every narrative, every parable, can be viewed through the lens of God's relentless pursuit of us and the continual invitation to partner in the divine vision of Shalom. In this journey, let us walk hand in hand through the gardens of scripture, feeling God's presence at every step. Amen.

 [1] Genesis 3:8, NIV

Reflect

I. Where do you feel God reaching out to you? How might God be calling you into deeper intimacy?

II. Consider the implications of being crafted in God's image. What does being made in God's image mean to you in everyday life?

III. Reflect on the responsibility of humanity as guardians of creation. How can you personally take action to uphold this divine mission in your surroundings?

Creator of All Things,
May we see your
image in us.
Help us to see your
love within and
be catalysts
for compassion.
Amen.

"

God persists in pursuing us, continually drawing us back

to the beauty & harmony etched into the fabric of creation.

”

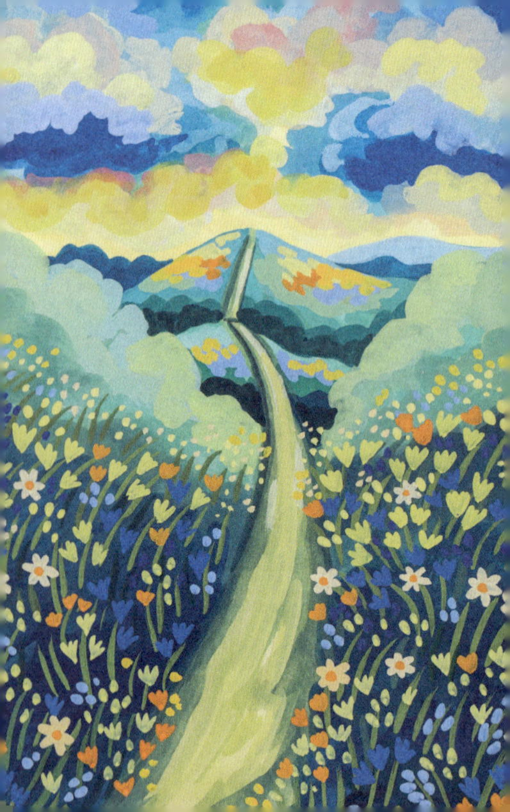

Divine Guidance & Provision

Synopsis

Isaiah's prophecies, rooted in a time of national upheaval, illuminate God's ongoing provision and guidance for humanity. We are shown the promise of a "Wonderful Counselor" and "Prince of Peace."

Reading Plan

- ○ Day 1 / Isaiah 7–11
- ○ Day 2 / Romans 3–4
- ○ Day 3 / Genesis 4–7
- ○ Day 4 / Joshua 6–10
- ○ Day 5 / Psalms 3–5
- ○ Day 6 / Job 3–4
- ○ Day 7 / Matthew 3–4

Read— Isaiah 7–11

The book of Isaiah emerges from a tumultuous period in Israel's history, marked by political upheavals and looming threats from the powerful empires of Assyria and Babylon. The nation, amidst unstable governments and self-serving kings, finds itself divided. The twelve tribes are no longer united but exist as the divided kingdoms of Israel in the north and Judah in the south. As uncertainty festers, many people yearn for stability and guidance, seeking it out in the false promises of strongmen and the imagined security of stockpiled resources. These things ultimately prove fickle, and in our passage from Isaiah this week, the all-consuming invasion by Assyria seems imminent.

It is amidst this chaotic backdrop that God's plans for Israel are revealed. Isaiah 9 radiates a beacon of hope and foretells the coming of a "Wonderful Counselor" and "Prince of Peace" to those in dire need.

This prophesied child represents more than just the vision of a brighter future; they are the embodiment of multifaceted, everlasting provision for all people. Amidst the most challenging circumstances, God reaches out with a guiding hand, offering hope.

Our lives are often complicated. As we navigate our way through the vast maze of life, we may falter or lose direction. We can fall victim to the notion that everything is meaningless, hopeless. Powers that seem so clearly stronger than us can leave us feeling trapped as we struggle to see a way out. It is into these places that God persists as our Divine Compass—an eternal presence, providing both wisdom and comfort, transcending even our deepest uncertainties. God is present with us.

Isaiah shows us that provision and direction from God are not merely ancient promises, but present realities that reverberate across the ages. From preserving Noah and his family through thunderous downpours to equipping the Israelites as they stared down the towering walls of Jericho, God reveals a path forward.[1] Isaiah's prophetic words demonstrate God's intention to provide for us continually, in perpetuity. The rescue promised comes to pass, again and again—best displayed in Matthew 4, where Jesus' travels mirror Isaiah's vision, showing history's hand at work.[2] Divine providence is not merely reactive, a band-aid placed over a particular wound. Rather, God is guiding us toward a better and more beautiful future in which the peace and provision promised in Isaiah 9 will have no end.

As we delve into the scripture passages for this week, may we be mindful of moments in which God invites all people into the divine plan. May we find true beauty, not merely in our final destination, but in the profound lessons, personal growth, and deep connections formed during our journey. With God's unwavering guidance, we can remain confident that, no matter the twists and turns, we are being led down the right path.

[1] Genesis 6–7 and Joshua 6, NLT / [2] Matthew 4:13-16, NIV,
 See Endnotes

Reflect

I. In what areas of your own life do you desire to see more of God's guidance and direction?

II. Reflect on the leaders and individuals facing turmoil in each of this week's passages. What are the qualities that drew them closer to God or pushed them away?

III. Consider the promises made and fulfilled throughout these chapters. How can these promises continue to bring hope into your life and the lives around you this week?

God who guides us,
May we remember your
promises in moments
where hope feels
distant amid chaos.
With your hope,
may we seek signs and
guidance on your
righteous path.
Amen.

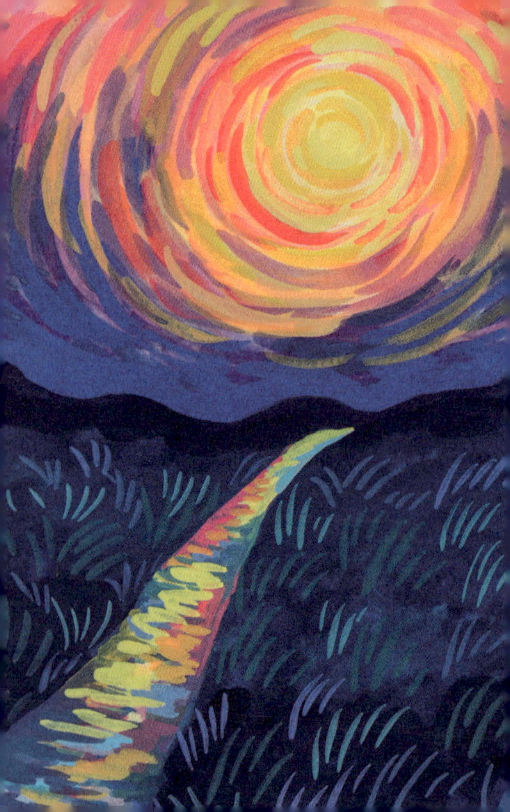

New Beginnings

Synopsis

We reflect on the notion of new beginnings through the lens of Romans 5–6. Paul encourages new believers to embrace a rejuvenated identity through Jesus, symbolizing the powerful potential of new beginnings in faith.

Reading Plan

- ○ Day 1 / Romans 5–6
- ○ Day 2 / Genesis 8–11
- ○ Day 3 / Joshua 11–15
- ○ Day 4 / Psalms 6–8
- ○ Day 5 / Job 5–6
- ○ Day 6 / Isaiah 12–17
- ○ Day 7 / Matthew 5–7

Read—Romans 5–6

In his letter to the Roman church, Paul offers encouragement and insight for the daily lives of these still relatively new believers. As they dig into their faith as a community, the echoes of what came before still reverberate. From previous religious practices and communities left behind, to past missteps and challenges, everyone has a *before*. It is into this place that Paul seeks to illuminate the new beginning made available through Jesus. He declares in Romans 6, "Just as Christ was raised from the dead […] so we too might walk in newness of life."[1] This message spotlights the rejuvenating power of faith and guides believers toward embracing their renewed identity in Christ.

[1] Romans 6:4, ESV

This reimagining is bold. It declares that what might appear irreparably broken or too far gone, seen so clearly in Paul's own *before*, can be transformed by God into something new, whole, and beautiful. Every aspect of our narrative can be refashioned by God into something new. Here, kintsugi, the Japanese art of mending breaks in pottery with gold, emerges as a poignant metaphor. Our pasts remain a part of us, much like the crack lines remain visible in the mended pottery. But God, the divine artisan, reshapes our fractured pasts into futures filled with promise. In kintsugi, the gold-filled cracks of restored pottery don't just repair; they create new and previously nonexistent beauty. Likewise, through Christ, we are recreated—the grace and resurrection power of Jesus continually mend the places where we are chipped and cracked.

We don't earn this gift; God graciously offers it as a new beginning. Scripture is rich with these examples of God's generosity. Genesis describes a world reborn under a rainbow covenant after the flood.[2] Joshua's passage into the Promised Land marks a transition from transience to stability.[3] In Matthew's account of the Sermon on the Mount, Jesus upends expectations about who is blessed, favoring the meek, lowly, and poor in spirit over the traditionally powerful.[4] God's hands overflow with fresh starts.

When we're stuck in broken, life-depleting patterns in our relationships with God, others, and ourselves, we discover potential for divine renewal. We're called to introspection: Where in our lives do we seek revitalization? How is our Creator weaving together our fragmented experiences? Through reflection and reading, we remain open to God's offered fresh starts, trusting that even paths marred by trials and mistakes are being transformed into landscapes of beauty and purpose. Amen.

[2] Genesis 9:12-17, NLT / [3] Joshua 11:23, NLT /
[4] Matthew 5:1-12, NIV

Reflect

I. Consider the areas of your past that still feel broken, hopeless, or beyond repair. How might you step into the newness made available and offered to you in Christ?

II. Reflect on how God, the divine artisan, has already worked in your life to bring about new beginnings and greater wholeness. Take a moment to recognize these transformations, and express your gratitude.

III. Think about how the trials and mistakes of your past have shaped your passions and purpose. How does this perspective influence the way you view these events?

God of new beginnings,
Guide us towards newness.
Mend our lives with grace,
and transform our lives
into stories of hope.
Amen.

"

Just as Christ was raised from the dead [...]

so we too might walk in newness of life.

”

— ROMANS 6:4

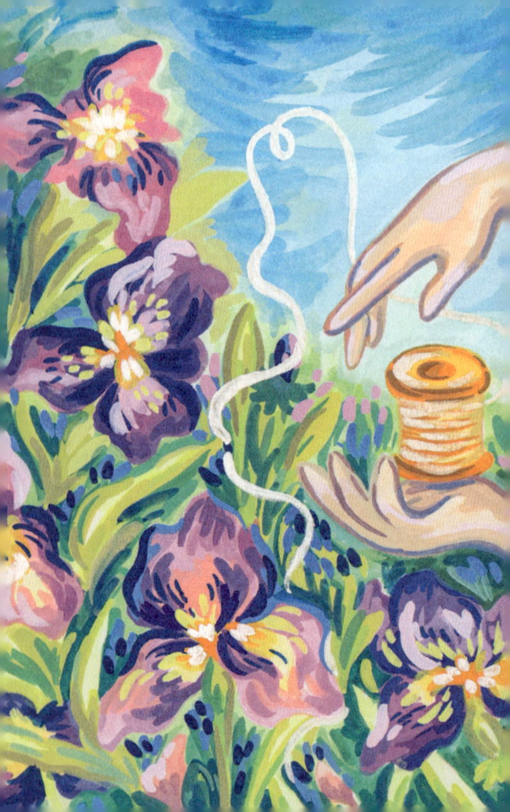

God's Unbreakable Promises

Synopsis

The story of Abram and Sarai in Genesis highlights the challenges and fulfillment of God's enduring, unbreakable promises despite human doubts.

Reading Plan

- ○ Day 1 / Genesis 12–15
- ○ Day 2 / Romans 7–8
- ○ Day 3 / Joshua 16–20
- ○ Day 4 / Psalms 9–11
- ○ Day 5 / Job 7–8
- ○ Day 6 / Isaiah 18–22
- ○ Day 7 / Matthew 8–10

Read—Genesis 12–15

In Genesis 12–15, we encounter the story of Abram and Sarai—a story about learning to trust in God's promises. When Abram and Sarai are called by God to leave Harran, God promises them innumerable descendants and great blessings, such that "all peoples on earth will be blessed through [them]."[1] Despite this assurance, as time passes, Abram grapples with doubt; Sarai's advanced age seems to believe the promise God gave them.

At a crucial moment in Genesis 15, Abram's uncertainty comes to a head. He struggles to reconcile reality with the vision of the future laid out by God. God responds not with ordinary reassurances but with a

[1] Genesis 12:3, NLT

binding commitment—a covenant. In that time, covenants carried a contractual connotation; they were legal agreements between two or more parties in which all sides agreed to uphold certain terms.[2] If either party breached those terms, traditionally, the contract was broken. Covenants required commitment from both sides to uphold their value.

But this passage does more than narrate a legal agreement—it unveils the steadfast nature of God's fidelity. While covenants made between humans can crack under pressure (as seen from generation to generation in the early chapters of Genesis), God's covenant with Abram stands unbreakable, irrespective of human imperfection, limitation, or expectation. God commits to follow through and make good, even if Abram falters or fumbles. The roadblock of age, which is impossible for Abram and Sarai to overcome, does not stop God from fulfilling the commitment to give them more descendants than they can imagine. And indeed, later in Genesis, Sarai (then named Sarah by God) will give birth to Isaac.

We catch further glimpses of the kind of faithfulness God offers in Romans 8, where Paul speaks of a love from which nothing can separate us.[3] Dependability like this is a staggering notion in a world where commitments often fluctuate. Yet, the covenant with Abram foreshadows the Gospel's climax: Nothing can impede God's faithfulness—not human frailty, the natural world, or any other opposing force.

God's promises not only defy natural convention, but also, through their miraculous realization, they reveal God's true character and nurture our faith. Miracles become markers in our story that we can hold on to as we navigate the obstacles of life. We see this displayed yet again in Matthew 8–10 by Jesus' calming of the storm and his healing touch to those who suffer. Across scripture, again and again, creation yields to the Creator's will; God's intentions are realized despite apparent impossibilities, and faith is strengthened.

In our shared reflections this week, let us meditate on the steadfastness

 [2] Genesis 15:9-18, See Endnotes / [3] Romans 8:39, NIV

of God's nature-defying promises—the same power that sparked life in Sarai's postmenopausal womb ignites hope in our trials today. May we lean into the powerful assurance of God's promise, a certainty not weakened by time or circumstance, and one that strengthens us beyond all earthly understanding. Amen.

Reflect

I. Do you sense God calling you in a particular direction? Have you experienced any obstacles in your attempt to follow God's call?

II. How have you seen God make good on promises in your life so far? How has this impacted your faith?

III. Are there any areas of your life in which God might be asking you to step out in faith and believe the impossible?

Steadfast God,
In your unbreakable promises,
we find strength.
Guide us to trust you as
Abram did, against all odds.
May we anchor our hope in
your covenant with us, forever & ever.
Amen.

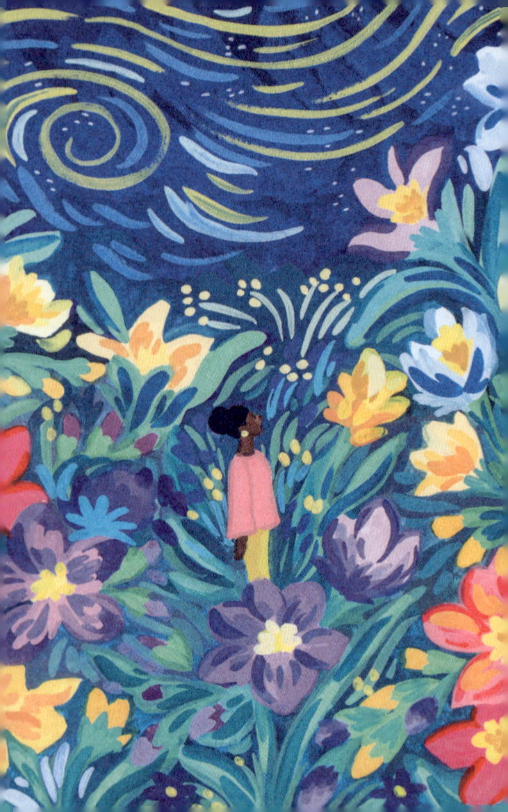

Trust in God's Unfathomable Nature

Synopsis

The Psalms highlight our struggle to understand God's mysterious nature and affirm how trusting in God's greater, unseen plan amidst life's uncertainties leads us to greater faith.

Reading Plan

- ○ Day 1 / Psalms 12–14
- ○ Day 2 / Romans 9–10
- ○ Day 3 / Genesis 16–19
- ○ Day 4 / Joshua 21–24
- ○ Day 5 / Job 9–10
- ○ Day 6 / Isaiah 23–28
- ○ Day 7 / Matthew 11–13

Read—Psalms 12–14

The Psalms reflect humanity's deepest yearnings for assurance and understanding. More than just songs, the Psalms are expressions of human curiosity and contemplation, constantly wrestling with the nature of a God who is both intimately known and profoundly mysterious. Spanning moments of joy and sorrow, celebration and fear, these ancient poems seek to make sense of a divine nature that doesn't always align with human logic.

Attempting to understand God's work is often like peering through a dense mist; we catch only glimpses of the true landscape beyond. The

[1] Job 9:10-11, NLT

intricacies of God's grand design often elude our human perception, shrouded as they are in mystery. Job echoes this sentiment, saying "[God] performs wonders that cannot be fathomed, miracles that cannot be counted. When he passes me, I cannot see him; when he goes by, I cannot perceive him."[1] God's ways are not our ways; often the path laid ahead of us feels unclear. Yet, reading the Bible confirms for us that, for all its ineffability, the divine plan is always working for the ultimate good of the world.

Living by faith means trusting that God's intentions go beyond what we can understand or see. When circumstances seem bleak and unsalvageable, like Hagar's fleeing to the wilderness, God sees us, opening new possibilities of which we never could have dreamed.[2] Even when the path is unclear, we can remain rooted in this truth: there is a greater plan unfolding beyond the veil of our limited understanding.

Psalm 13 shows what it can look like to exist in this nuanced space. Trusting in God does not prevent the psalmist from giving voice to confusion and sorrow: "How long, O Lord? Will you forget me forever? How long will you hide your face from me?"[3] But even still, this psalm reorients us in moments of uncertainty. The writer continues: "But I trust in your unfailing love; my heart rejoices in your salvation. I will sing the Lord's praise, for he has been good to me."[4] We are reminded that the goodness of God is eternal, even when it feels unfathomable.

When we attempt to fully understand God, we close ourselves off from the expansiveness of God's plan. Where we see boundaries and borders, God intends open doors and invitations.[5] Where we perceive lack, God reflects back bounty.[6] God is unfathomable, but amidst our awe and wonder, we can trust absolutely that God's plan is better than we could ever imagine.

[1] Job 9:10-11, NLT / [2] Genesis 16, NIV /
[3] Psalm 13:1, NLT / [4] Psalm 13:5-6, NLT /
[5] Romans 9:15-16, NLT / [6] Matthew 13:31-33, NLT

Reflect

I. Reflecting on your past, when have you felt unsure of God's plan? How did you respond to these feelings of uncertainty? How was God's faithfulness evident amid that situation?

II. How do you approach feeling uncertainty or a lack of control? How can you find beauty and wonder in the midst of these things?

III. Like the psalmist, how can we embrace both fear and faith, grief and trust?

God of infinite mystery,
Teach us to see
beyond our limitations.
May we embrace your
boundless plans.
In awe and wonder,
let us trust in you.
Amen.

"

But I trust in your unfailing love; my heart rejoices in your salvation.

I will sing the Lord's praise, for He has been good to me. ”

— PSALMS 13:5–6

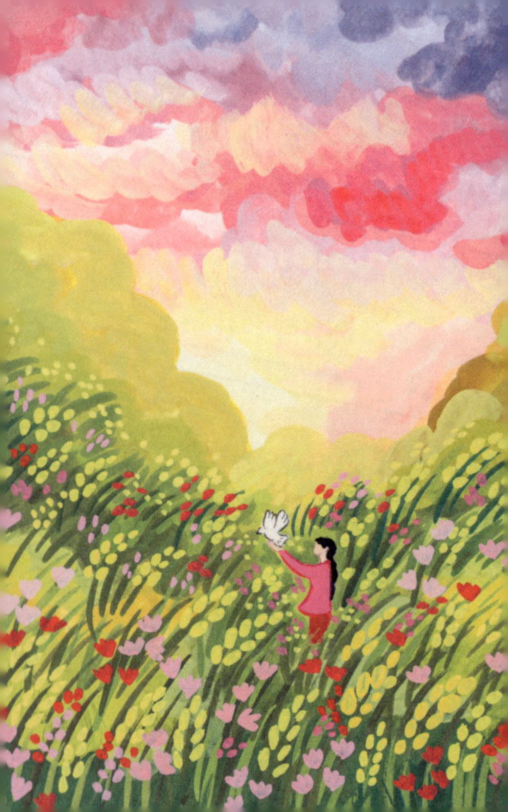

WEEK 6

Seeking Inner Righteousness

Synopsis

Jesus confronts the Pharisees' superficial practices in Matthew, redirecting our focus towards what true connection with God and authentic spiritual living looks like.

Reading Plan

- ◯ Day 1 / Matthew 14–16
- ◯ Day 2 / Romans 11–12
- ◯ Day 3 / Genesis 20–23
- ◯ Day 4 / Judges 1–6
- ◯ Day 5 / Psalms 15–17
- ◯ Day 6 / Job 11–12
- ◯ Day 7 / Isaiah 29–33

Read— Matthew 14–16

Matthew 15 presents a confrontation between Jesus and the Pharisees, powerful and pious leaders. Troubled and perplexed by Jesus' non-conformity to their standards, the Pharisees chastise him for his disciples' neglect of ritual handwashing, which they view as an essential practice for maintaining holiness. But Jesus redirects their attention from ceremonial rites to the intention *behind* such practices—"And why do you break the command of God for the sake of your tradition?"[1] With this question, Jesus steers the conversation from external practices to authentic spiritual living which leads to true connection with God.

Seeking inner righteousness is less about performative practices and more about embracing the virtues of love, mercy, and justice, as exemplified by Jesus. Here in Matthew, Jesus invokes the words of Isa-

[1] Matthew 15:3, ESV

iah 29: "These people honor me with their lips, but their hearts are far from me. They worship me in vain; their teachings are merely human rules."[2] In other words, if we cling to practices that are meant to orient us to the virtues of God at the expense of actually living out those virtues, we've missed the mark. It's akin to deep cleaning rather than stuffing our clutter into a drawer to create the appearance of tidiness. Stashing our mess away may create the illusion of order and cleanliness, but it rather misses the point of organization. Authentic faith is much the same, calling us to align ourselves with the core values Jesus embodies; to truly live out of love, generosity, and grace. Sometimes, truly righteous living can be complicated, messy, and may not always win the favor of those who would rather ignore the mess. But when we commit ourselves to embodying the values of God over and above the appearance of goodness, vibrant faith emerges that naturally impacts all aspects of our lives.

And what does authentic internal transformation look like? We see it in Jesus' ministry, in his willingness to break with tradition to reach out to those so often ignored.[3] In Job 11–12, we witness Job's unyielding integrity in the face of immense suffering and misunderstanding by his friends. For Job, righteousness is not merely about external composure but is deeply rooted in enduring honesty and resilience, even under scrutiny. Paul urges believers to pursue inner righteousness in the letter to the Romans, describing love in action.[4] These stories further urge us to thoughtfully reflect on our ways, challenging us to align our inner values with our outward expressions, embodying a faith that is both sincere and visible.

As we navigate the scriptures, we are invited to examine our own lives. Do we truly spend our energy to align ourselves to embrace the things of God? Let us actively pursue the deep, heartfelt righteousness Jesus teaches, making it a lived reality in every action. May this journey be one of genuine transformation that we not only seek but truly embody. Amen.

[2] Matthew 15:8-9, ESV; Isaiah 29:13, NLT / [3] Matthew 15:21-28 / [4] Romans 15:9-21

Reflect

I. What are the responsibilities and standards reinforced by others that prevent us from encountering Jesus and undergoing transformation?

II. What are the human rules that we find easier to follow than engaging in authentic true worship?

III. How can we create space to practice the virtues of love, mercy, and justice? How might we organize our lives around these virtues as a way of embodying inner righteousness?

Righteous God,
Let our words and life
reflect hearts committed to
love, mercy, and justice.
May we choose the
compassion and wisdom that
you embodied, and honor you.
Amen.

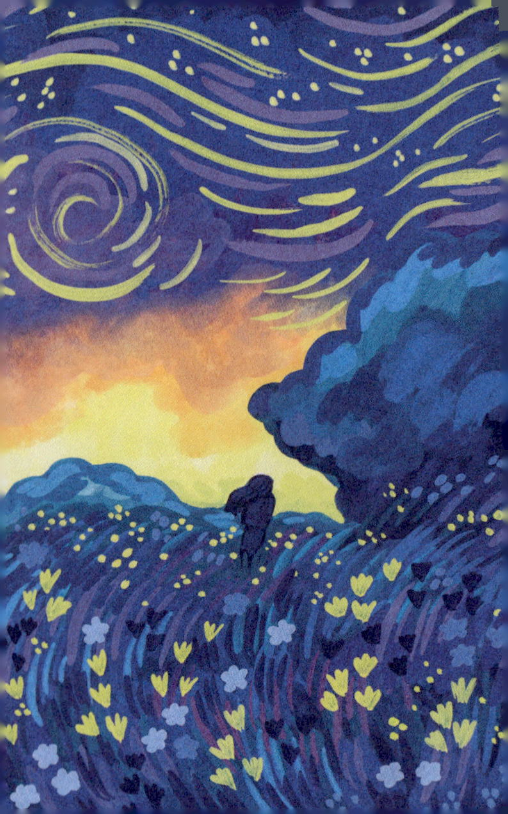

WEEK
7

God Delivers Us

Synopsis

David's life helps illustrate the nature of God's protective guidance and how trials can shape our faith.

Reading Plan

- ◯ Day 1 / Psalms 18–20
- ◯ Day 2 / Romans 13–14
- ◯ Day 3 / Genesis 24–27
- ◯ Day 4 / Judges 7–11
- ◯ Day 5 / Job 13–14
- ◯ Day 6 / Isaiah 34–39
- ◯ Day 7 / Matthew 17–19

Read—Psalms 18–20

Psalms 18–20 were written by David as psalms of praise following a period of great struggle. Pursued by King Saul, David was once fleeing for his life, and, accordingly, many psalms voice David's petitions and pleas for protection. God faithfully answers these prayers and delivers David from the threat of his enemies. Here, in Psalms 18–20, David joyfully celebrates and gives thanks, presenting us with the dual aspects of divine deliverance: God's invitation and God's pursuit.

Psalm 18 reminds us that God delights in our prayers and invites us to draw close. David recounts his cries to God and rejoices in God's faithfulness: "In my distress I called to the Lord; I cried to my God for help. From his temple he heard my voice; my cry came before him, into his ears."[1] This Psalm outlines a personal relationship with God wherein

[1] Psalm 18:6, NLT

God is not only a refuge but also an active deliverer, responding to our calls for help. David's experience assures us that God is with us and that God's deliverance is not a distant hope but a present reality. This is an affirmation further illustrated in Matthew 19 as Jesus invites a group of children, the most vulnerable and dependent among us, to draw near. God offers open access to protective and responsive care.

In addition to this invitation to dwell in proximity, Psalm 20 paints a picture of a God who actively pursues us. In moments of tumult and tribulation, God acts benevolently on our behalf. David writes of the myriad of ways the Lord reaches out to us, protecting us in times of duress as a force more powerful and dependable than chariots or horses.[2] This image of the God who pursues us is reflected in the Parable of the Lost Sheep[3]—in which the Good Shepherd goes after the single sheep who is lost, conveying God's unwavering pursuit of each individual. God is not a passive deity but, rather, a dynamic force in our lives, seeking us out in moments of distress and offering redemption.

God is tirelessly and presently working for our deliverance. As theologian Philip Yancey remarks, "Grace, like water, flows downwards [...] No matter how low we sink, grace flows to that lowest part."[4] Embracing God's deliverance means recognizing both aspects of God's divine intervention: the invitation and the pursuit. In the dark and difficult moments of our lives, we can turn to our Creator—bringing our worries, questions, and hopes to God, resolute in the knowledge that our cries are heard and will be answered. Even in the spaces where we feel unable to reach out, God is still there, ready to deliver us and delight in us.[5]

As we reflect on this week's readings, let us ponder our own relationship with God. By understanding that the Lord is at work in our lives, may we find comfort, assurance, and strength in facing our trials, knowing God's deliverance is at hand—now and always. Amen.

[2] Psalm 20:7, NLT / [3] Matthew 18:10-14, NLT /
[4] See Endnotes / [5] Psalm 18:19, NLT

Reflect

I. When have you experienced God's deliverance in the past? How did God protect you then, and how might God be intervening on your behalf now?

II. Psalm 18 references the Lord's righteous anger. Does this challenge how you typically perceive God?

III. Psalm 19 discusses how the earth and heavens declare the glory of God. How has nature revealed God's grace and intentionality to you?

God who delivers,
Help us find refuge in you.
Empower us to trust in
your boundless power
as we journey through trials.
Amen.

"

In the dark & difficult moments of our lives, we can turn to our Creator— bringing our worries,

questions, & hopes to God, resolute in the knowledge that our cries are heard & will be answered.

”

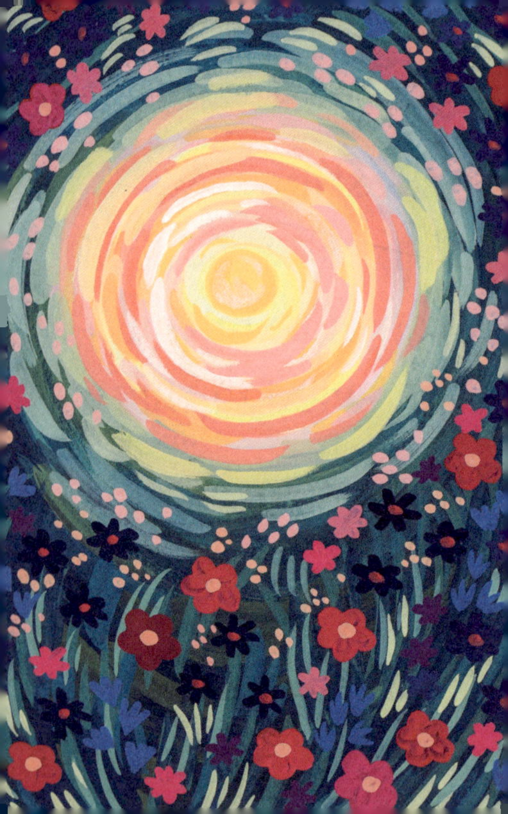

Heeding God's Calling

Synopsis

We explore what it means to faithfully answer God's call for our lives through the lens of Isaiah 40–44. The divine call rings out for all people with a universal message of hope.

Reading Plan

- ○ Day 1 / Isaiah 40–44
- ○ Day 2 / Romans 15–16
- ○ Day 3 / Genesis 28–31
- ○ Day 4 / Judges 12–16
- ○ Day 5 / Psalms 21–23
- ○ Day 6 / Job 15–16
- ○ Day 7 / Matthew 20–22

Read—Isaiah 40–44

Amidst societal upheaval and spiritual wandering, God's call for justice and righteousness thunders. In this passage from Isaiah, we are presented with a compelling invitation to join God on that journey, one that extends beyond the prophet Isaiah to all of God's people. "I, the Lord, have called you in righteousness; I will take hold of your hand. I will keep you and will make you to be a covenant for the people and a light for the Gentiles, to open eyes that are blind, to free captives from prison and to release from the dungeon those who sit in darkness."[1]

We see across scripture that God's calling goes out to all people, and is not bound by societal constructs or personal limitations. It reaches out to the marginalized, the forgotten, and even those we perceive to be against us. In Romans 15–16, we observe how God's calling over-

[1] Isaiah 42:6-7, NLT

comes cultural barriers, proclaiming the Gospel as a universal message of hope. It invites us to take on roles we might never have imagined, demonstrating the limitless and inclusive nature of God's reach. "Accept one another, then, just as Christ accepted you, in order to bring praise to God."[2] To embrace this calling, we must cultivate an openness to God's movement as we interact with people in our daily lives. Like Paul, who overcame initial hesitations to embrace a divine mission beyond his understanding, we too are encouraged to venture beyond our comfort zones and enter into a narrative larger than ourselves.

Sometimes, we may feel reluctant to answer God's call. There's a certain comfort in what's familiar; we resist anything that threatens to disrupt the balance we know. Heeding God's calling is a deeply personal yet interconnected journey, prompting us to explore uncharted territories, confront our inner struggles, and discover the potential God has imbued us with. But much like the so-called "hero's journey" defined by Joseph Campbell,[3] each step forward is a stride towards personal transformation and a closer alignment with God's profound plan. On the other side of this journey, we realize that what God has led us into is so much greater than the comfort we clung to.

Responding to this call might also be likened to embarking on a rigorous regimen of spiritual exercise. It involves honing skills to discern what God is inviting us into and cultivating the perseverance to continue, even amidst stumbles. Through this process, our hearts and minds sharpen, enhancing our ability to detect the divine in both the mundane and the extraordinary. Although realizing such a grand vision is fraught with obstacles, we can be encouraged by knowing that the God who has called us will also shepherd us the whole way.[4] And as the psalmist writes, the journey will include both difficult times in dark valleys and peaceful times of refreshment and rest; with God's staff gently guiding us back to the path when we depart from it.[5]

[2] Romans 15:7, NIV / [3] See Endnotes / [4] Psalm 23:1, NIV / [5] Psalm 23:2-4, NIV

How are we responding to God's call in our daily lives? Are we aligning our steps with the rhythm of God's expansive plan, or are we dancing to the same familiar tunes? May this week's scriptures guide us toward a life that resonates with God's vision for all of us. Amen.

Reflect

I. Have you felt "nudged" by God to connect with someone recently? How could you respond in faith this week?

II. Recall a time you stepped beyond your comfort zone following God's call. What changes did you experience internally and externally?

III. What practices could you actively engage in to help you tune into God's voice daily?

God who calls out to us,
Guide us daily to align our steps
with your expansive plan.
May we live in harmony
with your vision.
Amen.

"

I, the Lord, have called you in righteousness;

I will take hold of your hand.

”

— ISAIAH 42:6

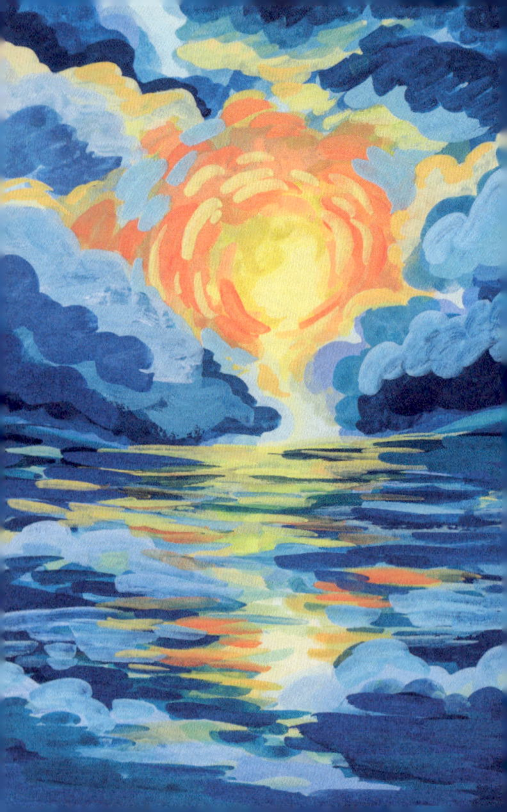

WEEK
9

Wrestling with Faith & Judgment

Synopsis

Jacob's wrestling encounter embodies the intense and transformative encounters with God that challenge and deepen our faith.

Reading Plan

- ○ Day 1 / Genesis 32–35
- ○ Day 2 / 1 Corinthians 1–2
- ○ Day 3 / Judges 17–21
- ○ Day 4 / Psalms 24–26
- ○ Day 5 / Job 17–18
- ○ Day 6 / Isaiah 45–50
- ○ Day 7 / Matthew 23–25

Read— Genesis 32–35

In this week's reading from Genesis, we explore Jacob's journey as he wrestles with both faith and judgment. Previously, Jacob deceived his older brother, Esau, stealing his blessing and birthright, then fled from his fury and retribution. Years later, apprehensive about reuniting with Esau and utterly alone and desperate, Jacob wrestles with a divine being through the night. This encounter transcends a mere display of strength; it is a catalyst for deep spiritual awakening. Jacob, who previously sought blessings through thievery and deception, now confronts God directly, seeking a blessing of his own.[1] This pivotal moment marks his physical and spiritual transformation; he is given a new name—Israel—to mark his next chapter, one defined by his relationship with the Lord.

[1] Genesis 32:26, NLT

At its core, this story is less about a wrestling match between two parties and more about a dialogue. Jacob brings the guilt and fear he has carried with him for years before God, seeking answers, assurance, and resolution. But amid this dance, this dialogue, God is equally present. Jacob emerges fundamentally changed and ready to confront and make peace with his estranged brother. Likewise, our faith journeys move us to confront our actions, our expectations, and God's place in them. We are invited to an authentic back-and-forth, bringing hard questions to God and allowing God to challenge us in return.

The notion of questioning God might make us uncomfortable. God is perfectly good and almighty. In the face of such a Creator, we may feel ashamed of our doubts and uncertainties and feel tempted to tamp them down. But as stories like Jacob's and Job's[2] remind us, God invites us to openly ask our questions; we will not be shut down when we ask why or urge God to intervene for us. And yet, this dialogue is not one-sided; when we wrestle with questions of our faith, we must also allow room for God to answer in ways we might not expect.

Wrestling isn't as daunting as it sounds. It is actually quite intimate. Author and speaker Jennifer Slattery puts it this way, "Wrestling with God is a sign of trust; a demonstration of intimacy & invitation for greater intimacy still."[3] So then, God welcomes us into this wrestling to deepen our relationship and reliance in regenerative ways.

Societal norms would lead us to believe that the natural outcome of Jacob and Esau's conflict is revenge. Instead, God enables forgiveness and restoration. As women in a competitive world, we are often lured into adopting a posture of competition and scarcity. But scripture shows us that rather than grasping for other people's blessings, we can rest assured that God has blessings in store for us all.[4] Instead of rivalry, God offers peace. God was the mediator between Jacob and Esau, the only one making it possible for them to truly reconcile.

 [2] Job 17, NLT / [3] See Endnotes / [4] Psalm 24:5, NIV

As we delve into scripture this week, may we enter into real and honest dialogue with God. Instead of wrestling with the world or ourselves, let us wrestle with our Creator. Let us give voice to our questions and uncertainties, and allow God to challenge us to embrace something bigger and brighter than we could have imagined. Amen.

Reflect

I. How does the image of Jacob wrestling with faith reflect your own spiritual challenges and growth?

II. How has God been involved in your conflicts? What impact has this had on your understanding of forgiveness?

III. How can you engage in a deeper, more honest dialogue with God as you begin this week?

God of Jacob,
Thank you for your authenticity
and closeness with us.
As we wrestle with you,
may we be transformed, and
may all blessings
follow in our lives.
Amen.

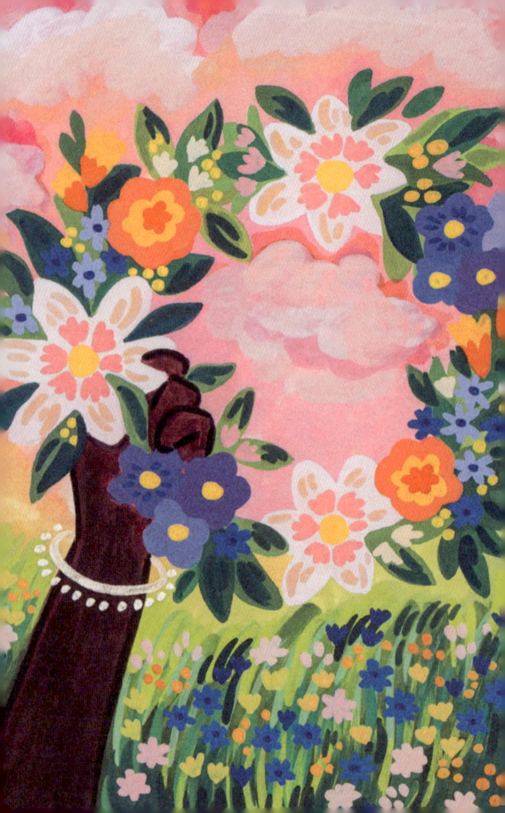

WEEK
10

Complexity of Relationships

Synopsis

The intricate dynamics of relationships are explored through the stories of Matthew 26–28, showcasing both the pain of betrayal and the strength of loyalty and love.

Reading Plan

- ○ Day 1 / Matthew 26–28
- ○ Day 2 / 1 Corinthians 3–4
- ○ Day 3 / Genesis 36–39
- ○ Day 4 / Ruth 1–4
- ○ Day 5 / Psalms 27–29
- ○ Day 6 / Job 19–20
- ○ Day 7 / Isaiah 51–55

Read— Matthew 26–28

Matthew 26–28 presents us with a mosaic of human relationships in the context of faith. First, Jesus and his disciples gather for the Last Supper. It's an illustration of community: praying, eating, and sharing with one another. Yet amidst this intimate scene, Judas conspires for personal gain; Peter faces a prophecy of denial. Later, in Gethsemane's shadows, the disciples sleep, leaving Jesus to pray in solitude. Judas' betrayal leads to Jesus' arrest, and Peter denies him thrice. The pain and loneliness caused by the shortcomings of The Twelve are juxtaposed with the loyalty and care of Christ's female disciples: his mother and Mary Magdalene. The women stay by Jesus' side to the end, witnessing his death and lovingly tending to his body afterward.

A wide spectrum of relationship dynamics are present in this passage, from profound loyalty and kinship to deep betrayal and discord. It is a powerful reminder that community is messy; it holds both beauty and conflict. Even in our closest relationships, we have the capacity to wound one another just as much as we can lift each other up. What does it look like to embrace the complexity of such relationships? What does it mean to extend grace to those we love, even amidst disputes?

As Theologian Henri Nouwen suggests across his works, grace finds its deepest strength in our commitment to mending what has been broken.[1] Restoration can be an intensive, emotional process. Like a bridge once collapsed, the path to reconciliation requires labor—clearing away the debris, acknowledging the breakage, and making a plan to rebuild together. Establishing new relational ties in this way means allowing space for human imperfection and messiness.[2]

We see this in Naomi's story in the Book of Ruth. Amidst profound loss, she adopts the name *Mara* to signify her bitterness. Her daughter-in-law, Ruth, meets her in that place of bitterness, unwilling to turn her back on this relationship. In response to Ruth's steadfast compassion, Naomi slowly opens up to the possibilities of redemption. Here too in the Gospel of Matthew, Jesus enters into our messiness and endures great pain caused by those he loves, but amidst that pain comes the path to restoration.[3]

In this, God models what healthy and nuanced relationships look like, holding us accountable while also extending grace. In the words of Isaiah 51:5: "My mercy and justice are coming soon. My salvation is on the way."[4] These passages, much like our own journeys of redemption, invite us to embrace complexity. We can experience the transformative power of honesty, patience, and perseverance in mending what's broken if we so choose.

This week, may we actively open ourselves up to the multifaceted nature of our relationships—with God and each other—as we find a path toward healing and wholeness together.

 [1,2,3] See Endnotes / [4] Isaiah 51:5, NLT

Reflect

I. How do the relationship dynamics on display in Matthew 26–28 mirror your own? What qualities can we emulate from Jesus' interactions with his disciples?

II. Consider Naomi and Ruth's story. How do commitment and compassion lead to redemption? How can you intentionally embody this in your relationships?

III. Reflect on Isaiah 51:5. What does it look like to pursue accountability with grace? How can you compassionately mend and strengthen your relationships in this way?

Lord of relationships,
Teach us to mend as you mend—
with grace for the broken.
May we build pathways
to peace for all.
Amen.

“

My mercy
& justice
are coming

soon. My
salvation is
on the way.

”

— ISAIAH 51:5

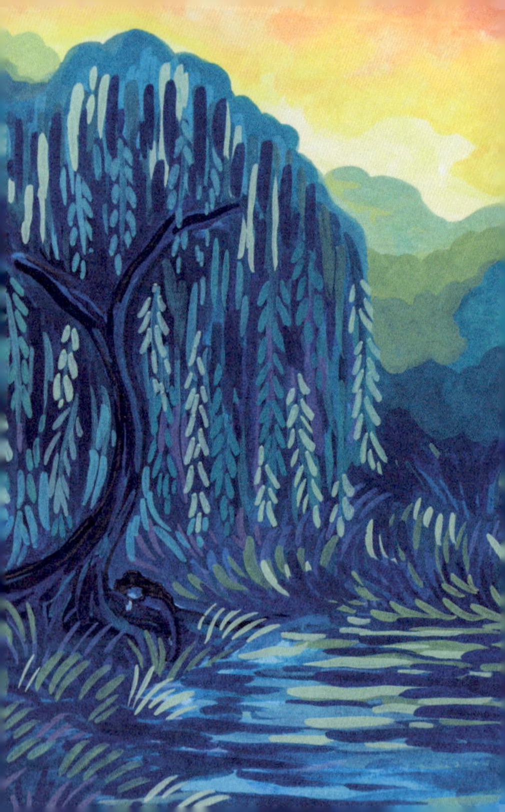

Steadfast Faith in Times of Sorrow

Synopsis

Through stories of great loss and despair, scripture illustrates the role of steadfast faith in providing comfort and hope amidst sorrow.

Reading Plan

- ○ Day 1 / 1 Samuel 1–5
- ○ Day 2 / 1 Corinthians 5–6
- ○ Day 3 / Genesis 40–43
- ○ Day 4 / Psalms 30–32
- ○ Day 5 / Job 21–22
- ○ Day 6 / Isaiah 56–61
- ○ Day 7 / Mark 1–2

Read— 1 Samuel 1–5

Our readings for the week take us into the heart of struggles. In 1 Samuel, we see Hannah's deep sorrow over being unable to have children. Joseph, in Genesis, journeys through unjust imprisonment, while Job continues to lament his misfortune. The Psalms present us with poetic responses to grief, while in Isaiah, promises are made to redeem the suffering. In Mark, Jesus heals those afflicted with illness.

These stories remind us of the raw edges of human suffering. Times of struggle prompt us to ask tough questions about faith. Is faith just a comfort blanket, or is it something that can genuinely guide and help us through deep despair? Beaten down and frustrated, Job seems

[1] Job 21, NLT

not to find the promises of faith compelling.[1] Amidst our own grief, perhaps we are inclined to agree. When the world feels bleak and dark, holding on to hope or assurance can feel like an effort in futility. However, God's caring and resolute responses to Hannah and Joseph suggest that faith is more than just wishful thinking; it's a solid foundation for overcoming difficult times.

Barbara Brown Taylor, an Episcopal priest, professor, and author, writes extensively about experiencing faith in unexpected places. In her book, *Learning to Walk in the Dark,* she explores the spiritual richness of navigating through life's darker periods: "I have learned things in the dark that I could never have learned in the light."[2] Taylor's reflection invites us to consider sorrow and difficulty not just as trials to be endured but as integral parts of our spiritual journey and growth. Hannah turns to God with her pain and longing and is blessed with a son, Samuel.[3] Joseph, wrongfully jailed, is enabled by God to interpret Pharaoh's dreams, saving not only himself but the entire nation.[4] God not only offers comfort in moments of despair but also moves to bring us through troubles. This is echoed by the psalmist who writes, "For you are my hiding place; you protect me from trouble. You surround me with songs of victory."[5]

Holding onto faith in times of sorrow reminds us that we are not alone and prepares us for the more beautiful future God has in store. Like Hannah, we might find ourselves hoping for something that feels impossible. Or like Joseph, we may endure long seasons of unfair situations where we feel powerless. Their stories are reminders that turning to faith isn't about escaping reality but finding a way to navigate it.

This week's readings remind us that even when darkness is all around, our faith connects us to a God who's listening and with us, joining us on our journey toward hope. Amen.

[2] See Endnotes / [3] 1 Samuel 1:9-28, NLT / [4] Genesis 40–41, NLT / [5] Psalm 32:7, NLT

Reflect

I. Reflect on the stories of Hannah in 1 Samuel and Joseph in Genesis. How do their experiences with sorrow influence your understanding of God's role in our struggles?

II. Job's story portrays a challenging perspective on faith amid suffering. How does his reaction to hardship challenge or reinforce your views on the importance of faith in times of deep despair?

III. Barbara Brown Taylor suggests that there are valuable lessons to be learned even amid hard times. Considering the readings this week, how can you apply the idea of finding spiritual richness in sorrow to your own life experiences?

God of Compassion,
Thank you for hearing our cries
and being our refuge in sorrow.
Strengthen our faith
with your promises
as we face the world's suffering.
Amen.

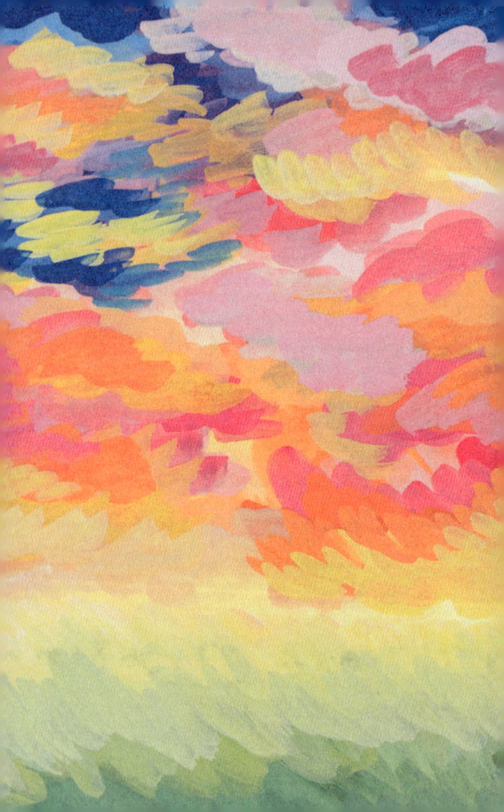

Anticipating a Better Future

Synopsis

Isaiah's visions prompt us to consider God's comprehensive plan for restoration and peace and how we can partner with God in shaping a hopeful future.

Reading Plan

- ○ Day 1 / Isaiah 62-66
- ○ Day 2 / 1 Corinthians 7-8
- ○ Day 3 / Genesis 44-47
- ○ Day 4 / 1 Samuel 6-10
- ○ Day 5 / Psalms 33-35
- ○ Day 6 / Job 23-24
- ○ Day 7 / Mark 3-4

Read— Isaiah 62-66

This week's reading from Isaiah offers a compelling picture of the future, where God's grace and vision dramatically reshape the world. Written during the Babylonian captivity in the midst of a season of great loss and upheaval, Isaiah's prophecy foretells a "new heavens and a new earth."[1] It's a prophecy of profound hope that promises total restoration—a radical vision. This is not a minor upgrade but a complete overhaul of all things.

What would an ideal world look like through our eyes? As we read about Israel's journey through exile, this prophecy stirs our imagination about renewal. We often think of progress in terms of material achievements and advancements. Yet, God's vision for the world delves deeper, aiming for a comprehensive restoration that revitalizes relationships, the environment, and our spiritual well-being. In this future, there is abundance for all—every need is met, from basic necessities like hous-

[1] Isaiah 65:17, NLT

ing, food, and healthcare to broader systems of support for children, the elderly, and the earth.[2]

On our own, our efforts to craft a perfect world fall short. We see this play out in 1 Samuel, when the Israelites demand a king, seeking a political solution to their spiritual challenges. They attempt to reshape themselves according to the world's conventions, neglecting their unique covenant relationship with God to be "set apart." They judge themselves according to the standards of neighboring nations rather than embodying God's vision for them.

In Isaiah, God responds to those who go their own way rather than participating in God's vision for change: "I will bless those who have humble and contrite hearts, who tremble at my word. But those who choose their own ways [...] I will send them great trouble—all the things they feared. For when I called, they did not answer. When I spoke, they did not listen."[3] Embracing God's picture of a better future means jettisoning our own plans and letting go of our desire for control. This lesson is further displayed in Jesus' parable of the growing seed in Mark 4. There, we are reminded that the farmer cannot control the growth or development of the seeds they plant, but they can participate in the sowing and harvesting.[4] The fulfillment of the Kingdom is in God's hands alone, but we are not confined to passive anticipation. As we look ahead to the future God promises, we're called to live imaginatively and constructively—advocating for justice, nurturing the vulnerable, and reaping the blessings to foster a harmonious community.

As we deal with today's challenges, no matter their size or strength, Isaiah 65 reminds us that we are not alone or without hope. God is at work, here and now, establishing a world where our deepest hopes for peace, justice, and well-being are fully realized. May we live in a way that reflects this promised future, joining in the work of God, and drawing closer to the world God intends for us. Amen.

[2] Isaiah 65:20-25, NLT / [3] Isaiah 66:3, 4, NLT / [4] Mark 4:26-29, NIV

Reflect

I. Where do we see God's vision of the future in the world today? How do you feel called to participate in making this vision a reality?

II. How have we tried to shape the world according to our own visions? How might God be inviting us to instead deliberately turn our attention towards God's plan?

III. Have you ever felt that God helped you in your time of need? How does God show up when you call?

God of Hope,
Help us face today's challenges
with the knowledge
that you are with us,
actively shaping a world of peace,
justice, and well-being.
May we live in a way that
reflects your promised future.
Amen.

"

God's vision for the world delves deeper, aiming for a comprehensive restoration

that revitalizes
relationships,
the environment,
& our spiritual
well-being.
”

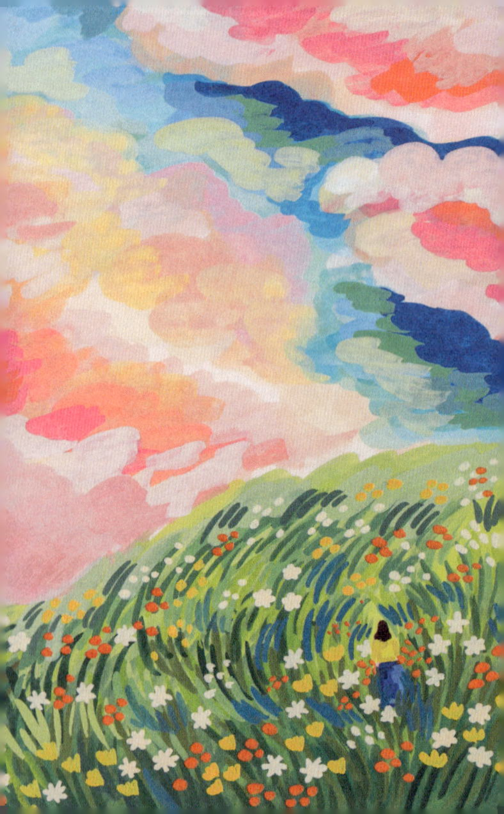

Learning from Past Lessons

Synopsis

Paul's letter to the Corinthians teaches us the wisdom of reflecting on our past through the lens of the lessons it taught us and how a life of spiritual discipline and growth deepens our relationship with God.

Reading Plan

- ○ Day 1 / 1 Corinthians 9-10
- ○ Day 2 / Genesis 48-50
- ○ Day 3 / 1 Samuel 11-15
- ○ Day 4 / Psalms 36-38
- ○ Day 5 / Job 25-26
- ○ Day 6 / Jeremiah 1-6
- ○ Day 7 / Mark 5-6

Read—1 Corinthians 9-10

The apostle Paul wrote 1 Corinthians as a letter to the Christian community of Corinth, a city in the Roman Empire known for its cultural diversity and bustling economy. Like our modern major cities, Corinth was a hub for a wide variety of beliefs, philosophies, and lifestyles, a challenge for those seeking to stay the course of their faith amid numerous distractions and societal influences. In this week's reading, Paul talks about life and faith in the context of a grand race; a race that lasts our whole life long. Amidst outside pressures and internal struggles, this race can be daunting. On some days, we stay the course, running with abundant energy and ease. On other days, it takes all of our focus just to keep from wandering to a path that seems easier, and all our energy to lift one foot after the other. On these days, the finish line can seem unreachable; but according to Paul, running the race of life to win is not about perfection, it's about intentionality. We are not running aimlessly but recommitting daily to keep traveling this road with Jesus and growing from the lessons we encounter along the way.[1] Each step forward, no matter how small, is a victory in this lifelong journey of faith.

To live this way is to learn from our experiences and mistakes. The challenges we face in our daily lives—pitfalls, obstacles, and unexpected turns—can easily throw us off course. Still, each day is an important leg of the race, so we engage with intention and determination; but on the days when we make a misstep, it is not game over. Rather, we are called to learn from these experiences, so we have greater wisdom and resolve the next time we encounter them. As Paul writes, "I discipline my body like an athlete, training it to do what it should."[2] Much like a marathon, our spiritual journeys require preparation, focus, and the ability to learn from each stumble to avoid future falls.

We are not the first to face challenges, nor will we be the last. The Bible presents stories of many people of faith who had moments of failure. Jeremiah recounts the people of Israel's turn away from God.[3] 1 Samuel 13 finds Saul trying to take matters into his own hands against God's instructions.[4] The hearts of Jesus' disciples remain hardened even after witnessing his miraculous feeding of the multitude.[5]

Likewise, each of us has mistakes and misdeeds that we wish we could undo. We need not be ashamed of our past. Instead, by reckoning with it, we come to see that God was with us through it, and God will continue to bring us through in the future.[6] In this way, mistakes become less like bad report cards and more like game tapes where we see where our actions went awry and how we can mend them for the next day's sprint.

As we enter into this week, let us consider the lessons we have learned from the past and adopt a teachable posture as we push forward into the future. May we meditate on scripture's wisdom, and, step by step, run with intention and focus towards the newness available to us through Christ. Amen.

[1] 1 Corinthians 9:25-26, NLT / [2] 1 Corinthians 9:27, NLT / [3] Jeremiah 2:1-13, NIV / [4] 1 Samuel 13:8-14, NIV / [5] Mark 6:51-52, NLT / [6] 1 Corinthians 10:13, NLT

Reflect

I. Consider faith as life's grand race. What pulls you off course? Are these distractions subtle or obvious?

II. Reflect on the last time you strayed from God's path. What did you learn from that experience that could help you grow?

III. In this race metaphor, how do you perceive God's presence? Is God running beside you, offering support, or cheering you on? Imagine God's loving accompaniment throughout this enduring journey.

God who is with us,
As we step into this new week,
may we carry the
lessons of our past
with a teachable spirit.
May we meditate on
scripture's wisdom, and
run with focused
intention towards Christ.
Amen.

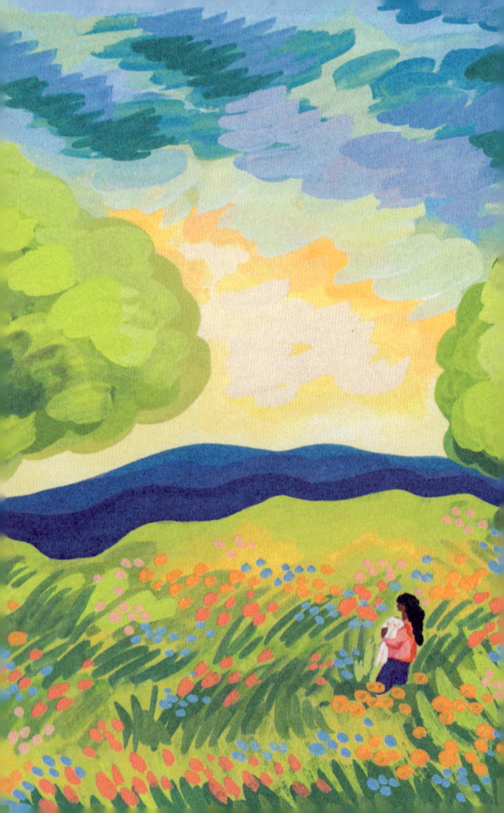

God Values the Weak & Vulnerable

Synopsis

We explore God's profound commitment to uplifting the downtrodden and marginalized across society through the story of God's rescue of the Israelite people from Egypt.

Reading Plan

- ○ Day 1 / Exodus 1-4
- ○ Day 2 / 1 Corinthians 11-12
- ○ Day 3 / 1 Samuel 16-20
- ○ Day 4 / Psalms 39-41
- ○ Day 5 / Job 27-28
- ○ Day 6 / Jeremiah 7-11
- ○ Day 7 / Mark 7-8

Read— Exodus 1-4

Exodus recounts the severe oppression of the Israelite people in Egypt. Reduced by Pharaoh to an economic resource, the people find themselves enslaved and exploited when it suits the king, and killed and beaten when they grow too numerous. Into this scene steps Moses, a humble shepherd, chosen by God to lead a monumental liberation. Through the burning bush, God commands Moses to demand Pharaoh's release of the Israelites. This journey of the Israelites from bondage to liberation underscores a key message: God champions the downtrodden, recognizing their worth and dignity, and bringing freedom to the oppressed.

Whether by witness or from firsthand experience, we know well how the vulnerable of our world are mistreated and undervalued. Individuals are too often appraised for their utility rather than as human beings with inherent worth. It draws to mind the famous words of Charles

Dickens' Ebenezer Scrooge, musing that those in need ought to hurry up and die to "decrease the surplus population."[1] Yet, we learn time and time again through scripture that God deeply values every individual, from the most wealthy and powerful to the Tiny Tims among us. The message is clear: each person, regardless of their social standing, is imbued with dignity and worth by our Creator. No one is "surplus."

Our world teems with contemporary Tiny Tims—individuals sidelined by societal structures, yet seen and beloved by God. As with the Israelites in Egypt, God is moved by their pain and desires their liberation. From unhoused people seeking shelter to refugees fleeing conflict, the divine narrative invites us to view each life as sacred, not as a statistic to be managed or an issue to be debated.

Psalm 41 reminds us of this invitation: "Blessed are those who have regard for the weak; the Lord delivers them in times of trouble."[2] We see this exemplified in Mark 7 when Jesus encounters the Syrophoenician woman.[3] Their interaction illustrates God's care and compassion for people traditionally deemed lesser. Jesus acknowledges her faith and heals her daughter despite societal norms that would have kept them separated. These scriptures challenge institutions and practices that exclude or divide us, urging us to actively uplift and empower the marginalized. God hears the cry of the oppressed[4] and moves us to respond in kind. For those in power, this means leveraging our position towards systemic change and building pathways for the upliftment of all. For those who have been cast aside or mistreated, this is an affirmation that God sees our pain and invites us onto a path of liberation for ourselves and for the whole world.

As we journey through scripture this week, let us carry the conviction that God's Kingdom is founded on compassion and empowerment for the weak and vulnerable. Let this truth reshape how we interact with

[1] See Endnotes / [2] Psalm 41:1, NIV / [3] See Endnotes / [4] Exodus 3:7-10, NLT

the world around us and inspire us to see the value in everyone, especially those whom society has easily dismissed. In embracing this divine perspective, we are invited to participate in God's ongoing work of redemption.

Reflect

I. With whom do you notice God's heart for the weak and vulnerable beating in you? Are there particular people or groups whose suffering especially moves you and ignites in you a desire for their liberation?

II. Reflect on areas in your life where you hold power and responsibility. How can you use this influence to bring greater freedom and dignity to people who are suffering?

III. Consider God's deep response to the cries of the distressed. How does this awareness free you to fully express your heart to God?

God of the weak,
You champion the cause of the
weak and vulnerable.
May we uplift those
often overlooked & partner with you
in your work of redemption.
Amen.

"

Blessed are those who have regard for the weak; the

Lord delivers
them in times
of trouble.
”

— PSALM 41:1

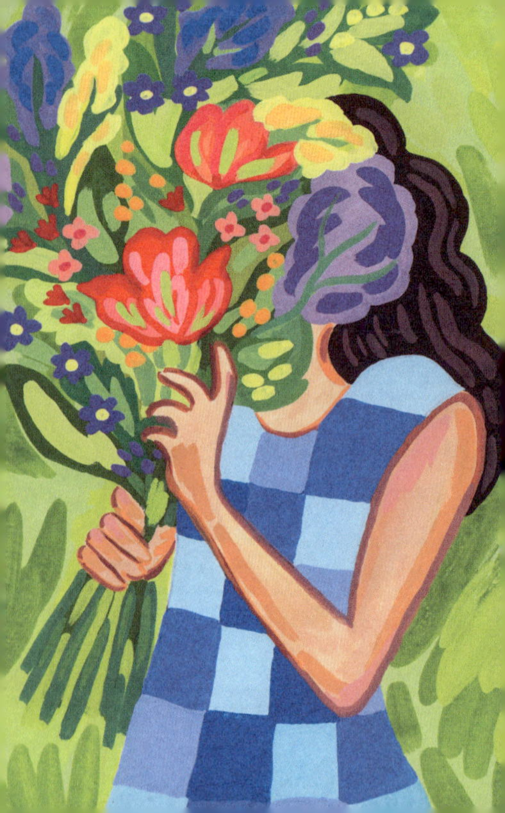

The Beauty of Serving Others

Synopsis

Compassionate living leads to a beautiful, fulfilling life of serving those around us. Jesus models this for us throughout his ministry on earth, particularly in Mark 9–10.

Reading Plan

- ○ Day 1 / Mark 9-10
- ○ Day 2 / 1 Corinthians 13-14
- ○ Day 3 / Exodus 5-8
- ○ Day 4 / 1 Samuel 21-25
- ○ Day 5 / Psalms 42-44
- ○ Day 6 / Job 29-30
- ○ Day 7 / Jeremiah 12-16

Read—Mark 9-10

In Mark 9 and 10, Jesus vividly models what it looks like to serve others, challenging his disciples—and us—to rethink our notions of greatness and purpose. In Jesus' words, "Whoever wants to be a leader among you must be your servant, and whoever wants to be first among you must be the slave of everyone else. For even the Son of Man came not to be served but to serve others and to give his life as a ransom for many."[1] Through his words and deeds, Jesus articulates a Kingdom in which extending help to one another is essential to our way of life, transforming competitive instincts into collaborative strengths. This call to service is not about diminishing oneself but about elevating communal well-being, where every action and choice can significantly impact another's journey.

[1] Mark 10:43-45, NLT

We see Jesus responding to debates among his disciples over who of them is the greatest. He introduces a child, a picture of vulnerability and dependence. It is in welcoming and caring for this child, Jesus tells us, that we best live into the Kingdom of God.[2] Here, Jesus inverts societal hierarchies by suggesting that true greatness lies in our willingness to serve the most vulnerable and to be guides rather than gatekeepers on the road to faith and community.

Being servant-hearted is not a posture reserved only for some. As the story of the rich young man shows, serving others is not about how much we can give, but the spirit in which we give. Jesus invites the young man to abandon his wealth as an invitation to de-emphasize personal gain and invest in communal abundance. This is a radical invitation to align one's resources and heart with the ethos of God's Kingdom, where serving others is intrinsically linked to serving God.

In perhaps one of the most famous of all Bible passages, 1 Corinthians 13, Paul outlines what perfect, Christ-like love looks like. He declares, "If I had the gift of prophecy, and if I understood all of God's secret plans and possessed all knowledge, and if I had such faith that I could move mountains, but didn't love others, I would be nothing."[3] When we love this way, we love as God loves us, not for personal gain or vanity but out of genuine care, by seeing and responding to the needs around us.

David's decision to spare Saul, eschewing vengeance for mercy, embodies this same Kingdom ethic. Rather than lording it over Saul with his power, David chooses grace, not only by sparing his life but also by showing him deference as a means of glorifying God.[4] This act of service moves Saul to tears. Indeed, a choice we might view as a weakness, Saul perceives as the strength it is—"And now I realize that you are surely going to be king, and that the kingdom of Israel will flourish under your rule."[5]

[2] Mark 9:36-37, NLT / [3] 1 Corinthians 13:2, NLT /
[4] 1 Samuel 24:6-8, NLT / [5] 1 Samuel 24:20, NLT

This is the beauty of serving others, a commitment to nurturing restoration, unity, and care within our communities. Through these passages, we see that service is not merely an action but a state of being, a way of walking through the world that reflects God's love and intentions for humanity.

Reflect

I. Reflect on the numerous examples of servitude in Mark 9–10. How might you challenge yourself to serve others?

II. Service, like that of David towards Saul, is not always convenient or comfortable. When you are presented with challenging service opportunities, what is your typical response? How might these passages encourage your responses going forward?

III. 1 Corinthians 13–14 talks of love and gives a specific example of serving a larger Church body in love. What differentiates loving service towards others?

Servant God,

Thank you for humbling yourself to demonstrate true service.

Guide us to serve out of love and discern where we can foster community through our actions.

Amen.

"For even the Son of Man came not to be served but to

serve others
and to give his
life as a ransom
for many.
”

— MARK 10:45

God is Our Refuge

Synopsis

Psalms reveal to us a picture of God as our great protector. This picture is further illustrated in stories from Exodus and Mark, showing how we can find safety and strength under God's care.

Reading Plan

- ○ Day 1 / Psalms 45–47
- ○ Day 2 / 1 Corinthians 15–16
- ○ Day 3 / Exodus 9–12
- ○ Day 4 / 1 Samuel 26–31
- ○ Day 5 / Job 31–32
- ○ Day 6 / Jeremiah 17–21
- ○ Day 7 / Mark 11–12

Read—Psalms 45–47

With its opening words Psalm 46 declares, "God is our refuge and strength, always ready to help in times of trouble [...] the God of Israel is our fortress."[1] What does it look like for us to make the refuge of God our home too? What must we understand to build our lives with God as the center?

Imagine a fortress—sturdy, dependable, and impenetrable. In times of turmoil, it stands as a stronghold, offering a place for collective gathering and protection. Its city walls tower along its perimeter, watching for all dangers looming from the outside. Inside its walls is a sanctuary. For residents, it has also become their home—a place where they

[1] Psalm 46:1, 7, NLT

live securely, shielded from external threats. This is the imagery called upon by Psalm 46 to illustrate the essence of God's nature.

God has our well-being in mind. When the world feels threatening, God shields and safeguards us, allowing us to navigate life's challenges with divine protection. We see this in Exodus 12, as God shields the Hebrew people's households from the plagues afflicting Egypt. Likewise, in Mark 11, Jesus fiercely protects the integrity of God's house, clearing out those who seek to turn the refuge of the temple into something self-serving.[2] The notion of the temple as a marketplace—a place in which people are separated according to their economic means—is a corruption of what ought to be a place of equity for all of us through our joint reliance on our Creator. God's refuge serves not only as an individual safeguard, but a communal beacon, drawing us together in divine love and grace.

This fortress is not just for one group of people but for all creation. Psalm 47 paints a vivid picture of God's all-encompassing power over the world, declaring, "For God is the King over all the earth. Praise him with a psalm. God reigns above the nations, sitting on his holy throne."[3] God is available to us all. Furthermore, God's invitation to seek safety in this sanctuary is not limited to times of distress but remains available to us as a perpetual dwelling. Whether in moments of great joy (as in Psalm 45), seasons of uncertainty (Psalm 46), or periods of fear and grief (Jeremiah 17), God dwells with us and we with God.

As we navigate the scriptures and our lives this week, let us consider how we can place God at the center. Let us hold onto the assurance of God's unwavering protection and embrace the peace that comes from dwelling in God's presence. Reflecting on these truths, may we find the strength to face each day with renewed faith and confidence.

 [2] Mark 11:15-17, NIV / [3] Psalm 47:7-8, NLT

Reflect

I. Take a moment to pause and reflect on your week. What would it look like to put God at the center of all your present circumstances?

II. How can trusting in God's promises of unwavering protection and peace help you recognize and support others who are in need of those same assurances?

III. Close your eyes and breathe. Imagine what a fortress might look like for you. Consider the ways God could be represented in its details, and keep this image in mind.

God of Refuge,
Be the center of
all we do.
May we cling to
your protection, and
draw strength from the
truth of your words.
Amen.

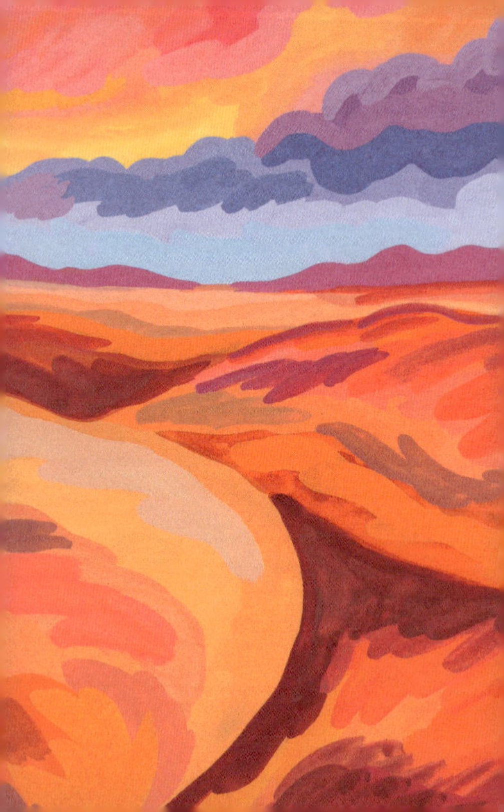

God is Mighty

Synopsis

We explore God's omnipotent nature through Exodus' dramatic displays of divine power and guidance, highlighting how boundless strength is made available to us through faith.

Reading Plan

- ◯ Day 1 / Exodus 13–16
- ◯ Day 2 / 2 Corinthians 1–3
- ◯ Day 3 / 2 Samuel 1–4
- ◯ Day 4 / Psalms 48–50
- ◯ Day 5 / Job 33–34
- ◯ Day 6 / Jeremiah 22–26
- ◯ Day 7 / Mark 13–14

Read— Exodus 13–16

In Exodus 13–16, we encounter the Israelites just after God has liberated them from Egypt. As they navigate the vast wilderness of the desert, God is with them the whole way. God guides them through the barren expanse as a pillar of cloud and fire, divinely parts the waters of the Red Sea, and rains down manna from the heavens to feed a nation wandering toward promise. With each leg of their journey, the Israelites come to know the might of their God, a might that holds them fast and puts all other forces to shame.

In our modern world, we are no strangers to the allure of power. Tech moguls, celebrities, and political leaders all wield significant influence over our lives. More often than not, however, it seems that those in power seek only to serve themselves and become even more powerful. They use their might to consolidate their control, buff their reputation, and line their pockets. But this kind of power is fleeting. Companies and individuals that seem indelibly powerful one day can find themselves outpaced or replaced the next day. Formidable empires turn out to be built on sand.

How does God compare to the forces of our world? The vivid scenes from Exodus demonstrate a power where God commands nature and lovingly provides nourishment from nothing. This divine action is not self-serving or vain, but purposeful and protective. God uses power to provide miraculously for an entire people's needs, offering sustenance, direction, and freedom.

God governs with wisdom and intention, acting with justice and providing generously. This week's passage from Jeremiah portrays God with the ferocity of a lion[1] and the force of a mighty storm[2]—elements that are strong, yet also protective and life-giving.[3] This imagery underscores the caring aspect of divine might. While worldly power is often inwardly focused, God's power is used for our good. Ultimately, the might of God is above and beyond human-made rule, and even the laws of nature. It extends beyond our comprehension[4] to every corner of creation. As Mark 13:26-27 puts it, "People will see the Son of Man coming in clouds with great power and glory. And he will send his angels and gather his elect from the four winds, from the ends of the earth to the ends of the heavens."

As we consider these passages, we're encouraged that God's might is not a distant or abstract concept, but an ever-present, guiding, and protective force in our lives. This recognition invites us to trust more deeply in this power that not only surpasses all earthly forces but also cares intimately for each of us. It's a holy mystery. God's might transcends our understanding, yet it is intricately woven into the fabric of our everyday experiences. This awesome combination of power and nearness calls us to live with a sense of peace and confidence rooted in God's ultimate authority over all creation. Amen.

[1] Jeremiah 25:37-38, NLT / [2] Jeremiah 23:19, NLT / [3] Jeremiah 25:34, NLT / [4] Job 33, NLT

Reflect

I. Consider how you typically view God's power. Do you emphasize its ferocity and transcendence, or do you focus on its presence in the small, daily events of your life?

II. Where in the world do you long for God's guiding protective power? Take a few moments to pray for the region, situation, or people whom God has placed in your heart today.

III. Reflect on how God provided for the Israelites in the wilderness. What situation in your life feels impossible? Take a moment to ask for nourishment there through God's might.

O Mighty God,
Your strength is ever-present.
It is the guiding force
in our lives.
May we open ourselves
to experience
your power daily.
Amen.

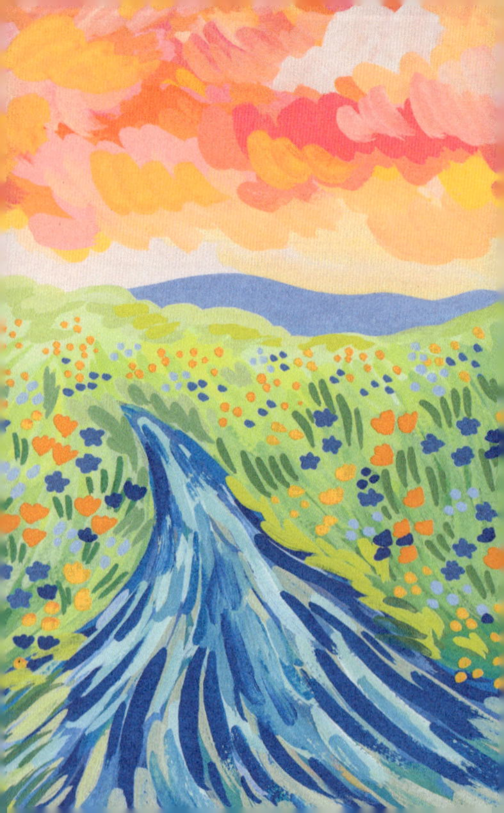

WEEK 18

Hope & Patient Expectation

Synopsis

We uncover the power of embracing hope and patience through the wisdom and warnings of Jeremiah 27–31. Together with the narrative of Mark 15–16, these passages teach us to trust in God's perfect timing for fulfillment and revelation in our lives.

Reading Plan

- ○ Day 1 / Jeremiah 27–31
- ○ Day 2 / 2 Corinthians 4–5
- ○ Day 3 / Exodus 17–20
- ○ Day 4 / 2 Samuel 5–9
- ○ Day 5 / Psalms 51–53
- ○ Day 6 / Job 35–36
- ○ Day 7 / Mark 15–16

Read— Jeremiah 27–31

In the fast-paced culture of the United States, waiting can feel challenging. It can feel like the only way to get the life we want is to go out and take it. Jeremiah 27 and 28 warn against the temptation to rush through life. False prophets, eager for quick outcomes, try to barrel ahead of God's schedule. Their actions reveal a deeper issue—a lack of trust in God's process. They want to force results, not understanding that God's plans unfold with great precision. Faith involves trusting in the deliberate work of God and believing that the divine is on the move in our lives before we see results.

In seasons of waiting, we might liken our lives to freshly planted seeds. On the surface, the ground appears dormant. Yet, under the soil, seeds are preparing to sprout. To try and rush the growth process can have detrimental results; we may disrupt the young roots or overwater the seeds in our haste for the harvest. In truth, all we can do is give the seeds what they need and let their process take its course. We wait in patient expectation for the seedlings to burst forth. This natural cycle of waiting and growth found in Jeremiah 27–31 teaches us about patience and trust in God's timing, even when progress isn't visible on the surface.

In Jeremiah 29:11, God speaks to the Israelites in exile with a powerful promise: "For I know the plans I have for you, plans to give you hope and a future." These words, delivered to a displaced people desperate for restoration, are not merely comforting—they are a call to action. They are delivered with instructions to build houses, plant gardens, marry, and seek peace and the prosperity of Babylon. Hope is not just an expectation, it's a way of life.

In Mark's Gospel, we see the ultimate example of divine timing in the story of Jesus' death and resurrection. The disciples, Pharisees, and crowds could not conceive that the suffering and death of Jesus were a part of God's plan. To Jesus' followers, his crucifixion seemed like a tragic end. To the religious leaders, putting Jesus to death was an attempt to enact what they believed to be God's plan. And yet, Jesus' crucifixion was part of a larger, perfectly timed plan that culminated in Jesus' resurrection, revealing that what might seem like an end was only a transformation. Salome, Mary Magdalene, and the other women who followed Jesus embody this posture in Mark 15. While aggrieved over Jesus' pain and unsure of what would happen next, the women faithfully stay by his side, trusting that God will ultimately show them a way through. God's timing, while sometimes at odds with our own, never fails to deliver its promised fruits.

What can we glean from the Israelites' journey with hope? As we navigate our own processes of growth—be they personal, professional, or spiritual—let's hold fast to these biblical truths. Like seeds planted in a garden, we are tended and cared for by divine hands for a vibrant unfolding. Embracing this season with hope not only offers us peace now but also prepares us for the joyful revelation of what's to come. Amen.

Reflect

I. Reflecting on Jeremiah 27 and 28, in what ways might you be tempted to rush through life's processes, and how can you trust in God's perfect timing?

II. Consider the metaphor of freshly planted seeds. How can you embrace the natural cycle of waiting and growth?

III. How does the promise in Jeremiah 29:11, "For I know the plans I have for you," inspire you to live out hope actively during times of waiting or uncertainty in your own life?

God of Expectation,
Thank you for our growth.
Help us embrace hope and trust
in your divine care.
May we be like seeds,
nurtured for a grand unfolding.
Amen.

"

For I know
the plans
I have for you,

plans to give
you hope &
a future.

”

— JEREMIAH 29:11

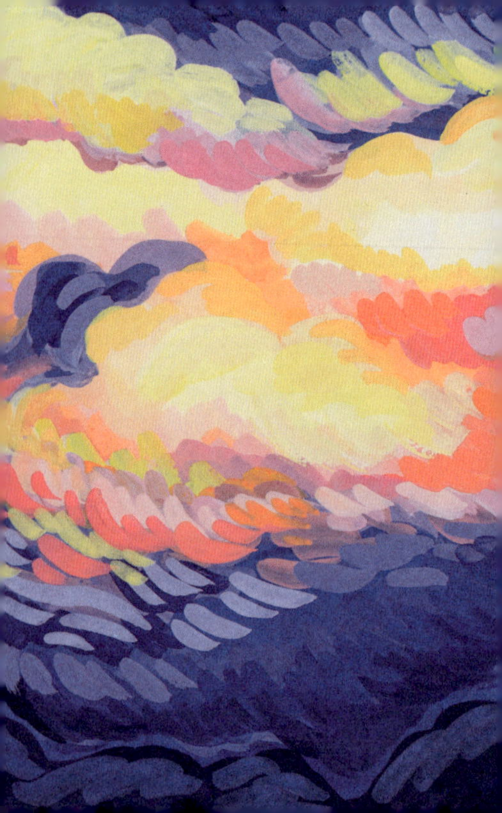

God's Vision & Plans

Synopsis

We explore the stories of Elizabeth and Mary, revealing God's strategic plans for humanity's redemption and the ultimate restoration of all creation.

Reading Plan

- ○ Day 1 / Luke 1–2
- ○ Day 2 / 2 Corinthians 6–8
- ○ Day 3 / Exodus 21–24
- ○ Day 4 / 2 Samuel 10–14
- ○ Day 5 / Psalms 54–56
- ○ Day 6 / Job 37–38
- ○ Day 7 / Jeremiah 32–36

Read—
Luke 1–2

When the Gospel of Luke begins, the people of Israel are living under tense Roman rule and occupation. For generations, God's chosen people had anxiously awaited their promised Messiah, the one who would mark the fulfillment of God's promises and plans. Amid this collective waiting, Elizabeth, a woman beyond the years of childbearing, is astonished when she conceives a child. This is not just any child but one prophesied to prepare the way for the Messiah. Her amazement only grows when her young cousin, Mary, visits and shares the news of her own miraculous pregnancy. Mary bears the Messiah himself, and God's great plan begins to unfold before their eyes, bringing with it a vision of restoration and peace for the entire world.[1]

[1] Luke 2:14, NLT

Mary and Elizabeth's stories remind us that everyone is invited to participate in God's plans. Although human beings often draw lines of division—due to age, status, or experience—God deliberately crosses these boundaries, choosing those we may overlook as instruments for Shalom—God's perfect peace. Elizabeth was considered too old, and Mary was poor and unwed, but both women were pivotal figures in God's redemptive work. The Lord's inclusive nature extends to us today. Just as Elizabeth and Mary contributed to the vision of God's Kingdom, we too are called to play a role in God's ongoing story, offering our unique "yes" through our time and abilities.

Yet participating in God's vision goes beyond individual interests; after all, God's plan is for our collective good. Across scripture, we receive a call to operate in community with one another, believing in "good news that will bring great joy to all people."[2] In this way, God's vision for the world is much like a community garden wherein every person, regardless of background or capability, contributes to the growth and health of the whole.

Scripture provides us with a guide for how to live out this vision together. Exodus 21–24 outlines God's laws and teachings on social responsibility, justice, and mercy. Likewise, 2 Corinthians 6–8 urges church communities to be faithful, generous, and forgiving. These instructions compel us as we move closer to the ultimate restoration made possible by Jesus. Relationships are central to our faith journey—a journey that is about more than mere personal salvation. In this process, we also seek the healing and renewal of entire communities, embodying the Kingdom of God so that love and peace can prevail. Thus, our daily lives and choices become acts of worship, contributing to a broader, divinely inspired communal life.

Where is God's plan in action around us? Just as Mary and Elizabeth were pivotal figures in the divine narrative, we too are part of something greater—a holy vision that transcends the limits of our understanding. May we surrender to joyfully living out God's purpose for us all. Amen.

 [2] Luke 2:10, NLT

Reflect

I. Elizabeth and Mary embraced God's vision despite uncertainties. How might God be calling you into something unexpected?

II. Reflect on Mary's Magnificat in Luke 1. How does this response to uncertainty resonate with your current experiences? How does it contrast with Zechariah's song?

III. Reflect on Mary's encounter with Simeon and Anna. How does their recognition of Jesus inspire you to embrace your role in your own community? What does Anna's presence suggest about individual contributions to God's larger plan?

God of Goodness,
Thank you for your plan
unfolding around us.
May we joyfully surrender
to living out your greater
purpose for us all.
Amen.

WEEK
20

Living Generously

Synopsis

2 Corinthians urges us to live lives marked by giving, compassion, and open–heartedness toward others.

Reading Plan

- ○ Day 1 / 2 Corinthians 9-10
- ○ Day 2 / Exodus 25-28
- ○ Day 3 / 2 Samuel 15-19
- ○ Day 4 / Psalms 57-59
- ○ Day 5 / Job 39-40
- ○ Day 6 / Jeremiah 37-41
- ○ Day 7 / Luke 3-4

Read— 2 Corinthians 9-10

Roughly one year after his first letter to the church in Corinth, Paul writes again to this community of believers. The city is a thriving metropolis, bustling with the likes of traders and philosophers, and adorned with opulent temples, noisy agoras, and lavish public baths—all reflecting Corinth's economic prosperity and diverse population. Amidst this backdrop, an early Christian community is growing rapidly. Paul addresses a letter to them, posing a challenging question amidst their opulent surroundings: What does it mean to live generously?

For Paul, being generous with each other is a natural outgrowth of God's generosity with us. "For God is the one who provides seed for the farmer and then bread to eat," he writes in 2 Corinthians 9:10. "In the same way, he will provide and increase your resources and then produce a great harvest of generosity in you." God, as ultimate creator, made all things and set the world into motion.[1] We are but a small part of the vastness of creation, and every resource or possession we have is a blessing from the Lord. Therefore, as an act of gratitude for God's faithfulness, we give because God first gives to us. Paul urges the Corinthians (and, by extension, us) to give freely and eagerly, assuring them that God will provide abundantly, so they can continue to share with others.[2]

2 Corinthians 9 emphasizes that giving is about the spirit behind our actions, not just the amount we give. When we choose to give without reservation or expectation, we deepen our connections to community.[3] We remember our shared purpose. Exodus 25 offers a vivid example of this: The people come together, pooling resources, to construct the Tabernacle.[4] As God's dwelling place, the Tabernacle is for all people, and so everyone has a role to play in its establishment. We might think of generosity as a river flowing through a community; it nourishes everything it touches. Through acts of giving, we cultivate a richer, more inclusive world.

The call to live generously is likewise reflected in the words of John the Baptist: "If you have two shirts, give one to the poor. If you have food, share it with those who are hungry."[5] Paul asserts that this sharing of resources has bountiful benefits. "So two good things will result from this ministry of giving—the needs of the believers in Jerusalem will be met, and they will joyfully express their thanks to God. As a result of your ministry, they will give glory to God. For your generosity to them and to all believers will prove that you are obedient to the Good News of Christ."[6]

Let this idea of cheerful giving inspire us today. Each act of generosity, no matter how small, is a step towards a more supportive and con-

[1] Job 39–40 / [2] 2 Corinthians 9:8, NLT / [3] See Endnotes / [4] Exodus 25:1-2, NLT / [5] Luke 3:11, NLT / [6] 2 Corinthians 9:12-13, NLT

nected community. Let us remember, every seed we plant was provided to us by our loving Creator. We are not merely giving away resources but giving thanks for these blessings and bringing forth a more beautiful world.

Reflect

I. How are you using your own resources to impact your community positively? Can you repurpose any resources to better support and benefit those around you?

II. Beyond financial contributions, what skills, talents, or resources can you offer to support those in need, such as volunteering or organizing community support activities?

III. What does generosity mean to you, and who exemplifies Christian charity in your life? Which aspects of their giving resonate most with you and align with Paul's description of generosity in 2 Corinthians?

God of Generosity,
Thank you for the blessings
you provide us to all of us.
Teach us to give cheerfully,
celebrating those around us.
All glory be yours.
Amen.

"We are but a small part of the vastness of creation, and

every resource
or possession we
have is a blessing
from the Lord.
”

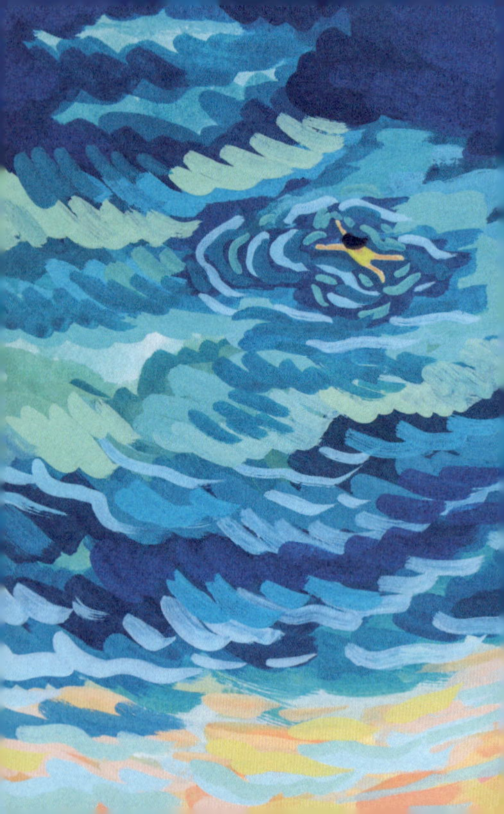

WEEK 21

God's Transformative Grace

Synopsis

In 2 Samuel, we explore how God's grace in our lives moves us from paths of conflict to peace. In King David and the apostle Paul, we find profound examples of renewal and restoration amid imperfection.

Reading Plan

- ○ Day 1 / 2 Samuel 20–24
- ○ Day 2 / 2 Corinthians 11–13
- ○ Day 3 / Exodus 29–32
- ○ Day 4 / Psalms 60–62
- ○ Day 5 / Job 41–42
- ○ Day 6 / Jeremiah 42–46
- ○ Day 7 / Luke 5–6

Read—2 Samuel 20–24

In these final chapters of 2 Samuel, we explore the twilight years of King David's reign over Israel. With his final words, David reflects on his journey, giving all credit to God for his victories and survival. David started out as the youngest son of a large family—he had no royal aspirations. But God altered his path. David's rule, although marked by significant achievements, also included profound missteps, notably his abuse of Bathsheba and Uriah and the ensuing personal and political fallout.[1] Yet, David recounts experiencing God's boundless mercy and restoration. He acknowledges that his story is part of a larger divine plan, one that seeks to graciously transform individuals regardless of their past or perceived insignificance.

God not only opens a path forward through divine grace but also brings

[1] 2 Samuel 11–12, NLT, See Endnotes

restoration to every part of our lives. What we perceive as weaknesses or dead ends—whether it's a career setback, a strained relationship, or a personal struggle—God can transform into strengths and possibilities. The opposing force to grace is the expectation of perfection. We strive for a standard we can never achieve on our own and feel overcome by shame when we fall short. But God doesn't write us off for mistakes and is infinitely patient with us in the process of restoration and redemption. No one is too far gone or too small to be part of God's divine plan, which manifests its wonders through even the most unexpected sources.

If we think of God as a bridge builder, then God's grace is the bridge itself—sturdy and reliable, spanning the gap over the vast and seemingly uncrossable ravines in our lives. With God's grace as our bridge, no obstacle is too great, and there is always a way forward. The Bible is filled with stories reflecting God's transformative grace. The apostle Paul, once the persecutor known as Saul, speaks of his divine transformation thusly: "Three times I pleaded with the Lord to take [my struggles] away from me. But he said to me, 'My grace is sufficient for you, for my power is made perfect in weakness.'"[2] After immense and unexpected suffering, Job is restored to prosperity and joy. Amidst his ordeal, Job felt hopeless and forsaken, but he comes to understand that God was by his side all along.[3] Job's restoration highlights that no purpose of God can be thwarted, teaching us that God's redemptive plan is often beyond our understanding.

The ministry of Jesus, as recounted in the Gospel of Luke, likewise extends this vision of divine grace. Through healing the marginalized, loving his enemies, and eating and associating with so-called sinners, Jesus presents the profound paradigm shift of the Gospel, moving us from strict adherence to the letter of the law to a spirit of love, forgiveness, and inclusion. In Jesus' example, we come to understand that God's grace not only bridges but also rebuilds. Grace is more than a mere second chance; it is a lifelong restorative process, turning every challenge into a testimony of faith and every individual story into a chapter of a grander narrative of salvation.

 [2] 2 Corinthians 12:8-9, NIV / [3] Job 42:1-3, NLT

Let us hold these truths close as we navigate our own valleys and peaks, knowing that with God, every end can be a new beginning. May we move forward with faith, trusting in the perfect architect of our lives. Amen.

Reflect

I. Take a moment to meditate on what it means to be human. What are our limitations? How do we fall short? Then, reflect on the human ability to change, grow, and heal.

II. Think of a time when you experienced shame. How might you invite God's grace for you into that moment?

III. Consider how God is able to hold people accountable while offering them grace amidst mistakes. How can you offer this kind of grace to the challenging people in your life?

God,

Thank you for your grace
which transforms our
weaknesses into strengths.
Let us trust in you,
to rebuild and renew us, and
help us begin again.
Amen.

"My grace is sufficient for you, for my

power is
made perfect
in weakness.
”

— 2 CORINTHIANS 12:9

Pursuing Wisdom

Synopsis

We explore what it means to live wisely according to the Book of Proverbs. True wisdom urges us to keep our hearts and minds open to God's guidance and instruction.

Reading Plan

- ◯ Day 1 / Proverbs 1
- ◯ Day 2 / Galatians 1–3
- ◯ Day 3 / Exodus 33–36
- ◯ Day 4 / 1 Kings 1–4
- ◯ Day 5 / Psalms 63–65
- ◯ Day 6 / Jeremiah 47–52
- ◯ Day 7 / Luke 7–8

Read— Proverbs 1

As the Book of Proverbs opens, Solomon writes, "The fear of the Lord is the beginning of knowledge; fools despise wisdom and instruction."[1] Wisdom is personified as a figure standing firmly at the gates of a bustling city. She calls to those passing by, her voice cutting through the daily noise: "How long, O simple ones, will you love being simple?"[2] Proverbs paints a sharp delineation between those who pause to listen, seeking knowledge, and the fools who ignore wisdom's call. To live wisely is to live according to God's direction; it is a life characterized by prudence, humility, and care. The stark warnings in this dramatic introduction illustrate the vital importance of opening ourselves to divine instruction.

Scripture presents wisdom not as an ephemeral notion but as a *person* who calls us into relationship, seeking to mentor us in her ways. The

[1] Proverbs 1:7, ESV / [2] Proverbs 1:22, ESV

Book of Proverbs guides us in developing our ability to pay attention so we can discern the wisest path forward, a path that invariably honors and glorifies God. It encourages us to attune ourselves to the subtleties of God's voice in a world that often overwhelms us with its volume.

What does it look like to live wisely amidst the cacophony of life's demands and distractions? We might imagine an angler waiting patiently on still water to catch a fish. Like our quest for wisdom, fishing requires stillness, patience, and a readiness to act when the moment arrives. The angler knows that beneath the calm surface, the waters are teeming with life. Similarly, we are reminded that beneath the regular rhythms of our daily routines lies rich depths of knowledge to be explored. In this stillness and quiet, we find that patience leads to better results than hurried action. When we rush forward without pause, we risk missing the subtle wisdom that invites us to move thoughtfully and purposefully through the world.

Pursuing true wisdom isn't about proving ourselves the smartest or most successful. Rather, to be wise is to follow the path God sets out for us, keeping our eyes fixed on the divine and not getting distracted by the ways of the world. In Psalm 6[3], this is expressed as a profound longing: "You, God, are my God, earnestly I seek you; I thirst for you, my whole being longs for you."[3] Solomon exemplifies this posture in 1 Kings 2 when he becomes king. He prays not for wealth or longevity but for the wisdom and discernment to govern his people effectively—a humble approach that shows real wisdom involves recognizing our limitations and seeking God's guidance above all. It's like the good soil that Jesus talks about in Luke 8, the soil of a heart that hears God's words and clings to it.

As we reflect on this week's teachings, let's carry with us the image of the angler—her patience and her attunement to the environment. May we learn to embrace the quiet, the stillness, that allows us to hear wisdom's call. Let this week be one of mindful observation and deep listening, where we seek not just to hear but to understand and apply the

 [3] Psalm 63:1, NIV

wisdom that calls to us in the midst of our daily lives. In doing so, we honor the divine path set before us, navigating our days with the discernment and grace that God offers.

Reflect

I. What does yearning look like to you? In what ways can you embody a deep yearning for God?

II. What positive impacts could embracing wisdom's call have on your everyday thoughts and actions?

III. What practices can you adopt to cultivate a life of wisdom? How can you implement those practices this week?

God of Wisdom,
Guide us to embrace the
stillness that reveals your voice.
Help us to live wisely and
humbly along the path you've
laid out for us.
Amen.

WEEK 23

Extending Hospitality

Synopsis

These chapters from the Gospel of Luke invite us to reflect on the notion of hospitality in our lives. Jesus' teachings illuminate what it means for us to truly love our neighbors.

Reading Plan

- ○ Day 1 / Luke 9–10
- ○ Day 2 / Galatians 4–6
- ○ Day 3 / Exodus 37–40
- ○ Day 4 / 1 Kings 5–9
- ○ Day 5 / Psalms 66–68
- ○ Day 6 / Proverbs 2–3
- ○ Day 7 / Lamentations

Read—Luke 9–10

In Luke 9 and 10, we encounter a collection of stories that explore the notion of hospitality. From Jesus' visit to Mary and Martha to the parable of the Good Samaritan to the miraculous feeding of crowds, these chapters invite us to consider the question "What does it mean to be truly hospitable?" When Jesus visits the home of Martha and Mary, Martha busies herself with the logistical preparations to serve their guest. But Mary sits attentively at Jesus' feet, absorbing his teachings. Meanwhile, the parable of the Good Samaritan tells the story of a man who is robbed and left injured by the roadside. A priest and a Levite pass by without offering help, but a Samaritan man, moved with compassion, stops to assist him. He provides immediate aid and ensures the man's continued care at an inn. In both stories, we see a picture of hospitality that is proactive and sacrificial, centering the humanity of those who are welcomed.

Martha's efforts to host Jesus underscore a common challenge in practicing hospitality: balancing active service with a direct, personal presence with one's guests. While she diligently prepares the home, her preoccupation with her tasks prevents her from fully engaging with Jesus, and she misses a moment ripe for listening and connection. While well-intentioned, her preoccupation with hosting has become a barrier to authentically seeing and engaging with her guest. In contrast, Mary exemplifies the core of hospitality by being fully present with Jesus, absorbing his words and teachings.

Seeing is indeed the necessary first step to extending hospitality. Mary sees Jesus; the Samaritan sees the injured man. But seeing involves more than just looking with our eyes. Truly seeing someone means responding to their needs with empathy and kindness, listening closely to what they require or desire from us, rather than assuming we know what they need. Hospitality, in its essence, is an extension of our love for God—a love that compels us to care for others with the same attentive care we receive from God.

We see another misguided attempt at hospitality when Peter witnesses the Transfiguration, and his immediate reaction is to build shelters for Jesus, Moses, and Elijah. It's a gesture that, like Martha's busyness, prioritizes an outward display of care over presence.[1] As Galatians 6:2 urges, "Carry each other's burdens, and in this way you will fulfill the law of Christ." Extending hospitality is not about self-aggrandizement but selfless service, recognizing our neighbors as valuable members of a shared community, and supporting and uplifting one another.

As we reflect on the parable of the Good Samaritan, we recognize that everyone we encounter is our neighbor. Jesus invites and empowers us to extend love and hospitality far beyond conventional expectations, to truly embody the principle of "love your neighbor as yourself."[2] And the first step of extending this hospitality is asking God to open

 [1] Luke 9:33, NLT / [2] Luke 10:27, NLT

our eyes and hearts so we can truly see and be present to the people around us.

Reflect

I. Reflect on a time you felt truly seen and welcomed by someone who extended hospitality to you. What did they do or say that let you know they were present with you? How does this relate to God's presence and attention towards you?

II. Has someone crossed your path that you sense the Holy Spirit calling you to extend hospitality towards? What would it look like to take the first step, to offer your presence and attention?

III. How might you be present to God this week? Is there a time or space that, like Mary, you can sit at Jesus' feet listening?

Welcoming God,
Thank you for seeing us
and empowering us to love.
May we be present
to our neighbors and
tend to each other's burdens.
Amen.

"

Carry each other's burdens, & in this

way you
will fulfill
the law of
Christ.

”

— GALATIANS 6:2

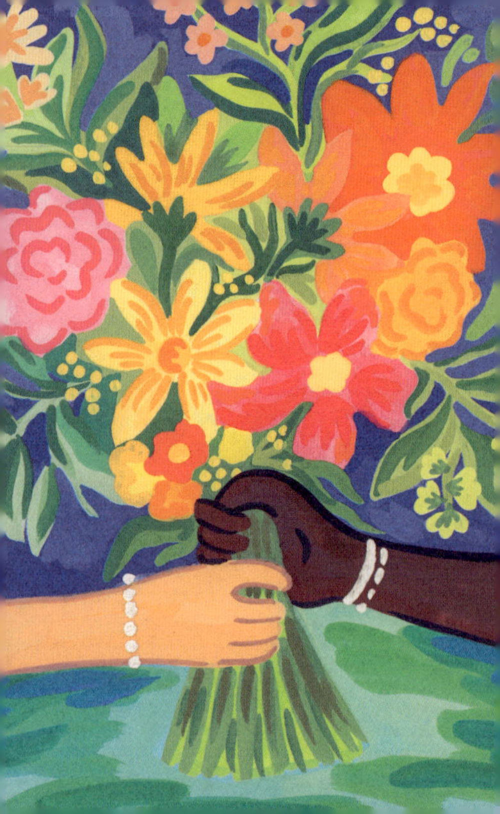

Unity Through Inclusion

Synopsis

Paul's letter to the Ephesians calls us towards unity—one that transcends cultural and social barriers and reflects God's Kingdom on earth.

Reading Plan

- ○ Day 1 / Ephesians 1–3
- ○ Day 2 / Leviticus 1–3
- ○ Day 3 / 1 Kings 10–13
- ○ Day 4 / Psalms 69–71
- ○ Day 5 / Proverbs 4
- ○ Day 6 / Ezekiel 1–6
- ○ Day 7 / Luke 11–12

Read—Ephesians 1–3

Amidst the bustling diversity and multiculturalism of the Roman Empire, apostles like Paul and Timothy travel far and wide sharing the good news of the Gospel. The early Christian church itself reflects this diversity, made up of Jewish and Hellenistic believers both. It's in this context that the Letter to the Ephesians is written. Many scholars believe that Ephesians was an epistle intended to be circulated around to numerous faith communities, with broad themes as applicable to the believers in Ephesus as to us today. Noticing a tendency for believers to segregate themselves across cultural lines, Paul writes to offer guidance in what it means to be a united community following Jesus.

In Paul's words, "Christ himself has brought peace to us. He united Jews and Gentiles into one people when, in his own body on the cross, he broke down the wall of hostility that separated us."[1] The barriers that we erect amongst each other are dismantled by Jesus; the divides that once seemed uncrossable are made insignificant by God's uniting love and grace. "Now all of us can come to the Father through the same Holy Spirit because of what Christ has done for us" (Ephesians 2:18, NLT). Our shared identity as children of God and our shared need for God's mercy[2] become the most essential part of us and therefore, we stand united.

The call for unity is not exclusive to the New Testament; it is an ever-present vision for humanity God has been inviting us into throughout our history. We see connections built and relationships developed across regional and cultural boundaries in the account of Solomon and the Queen of Sheba in 1 Kings 10, as shared respect and admiration for God lead to common understanding. Psalm 69 highlights the pain that exclusion can cause, affirming that separation and division are not what God desires of us.[3]

But importantly, unity does not demand uniformity. Our shared identity in Christ serves as the foundation of our unity, yet it is our differences that enhance our community's functionality and beauty. Much like a house is made up of different rooms, each serving a specific purpose, the Church is enriched by the diversity of its members. Each person brings their own "room"—their experiences, talents, and perspectives—into the larger "house" of God's Kingdom. Just as a house composed solely of kitchens would lack functionality, a community without diversity would miss out on the full richness of its collective potential. In Christ, we find the capacity to appreciate and celebrate these distinctions, knowing that it is our shared redemption and love from God that truly unites us. As Jesus says, "For everyone who asks, receives. Everyone who seeks finds. And to everyone who knocks, the door will be opened."[4]

Let us consider our communities this week, meditating on the barriers we may inadvertently build and how, like Christ, we might work to tear them down, not just with our words but through our actions. May

[1] Ephesians 2:14, NLT / [2] See Endnotes /
 [3] Psalm 69:4-12, NLT / [4] Luke 11:10, NLT

we find strength in our common faith and enrich each other by celebrating our differences, drawing closer to the unity that God envisions for us all.

Reflect

I. Reflect on the ways your community fosters unity through inclusion. Does it celebrate individual uniqueness or tend towards assimilation?

II. Consider how building relationships with those different from you has shaped your faith journey. What positive impacts have you noticed?

III. Where might God be encouraging you to break down walls of indifference and division to foster deeper connections?

Unifying God,
Thank you for
valuing our uniqueness.
Guide us to break down barriers,
honor everyone in our
community, and deepen our
love for one another.
Amen.

"

Christ himself has brought peace to us. He united Jews & Gentiles into one people when, in his own body on the cross, he broke down the wall of hostility that separated us.

”

— EPHESIANS 2:14

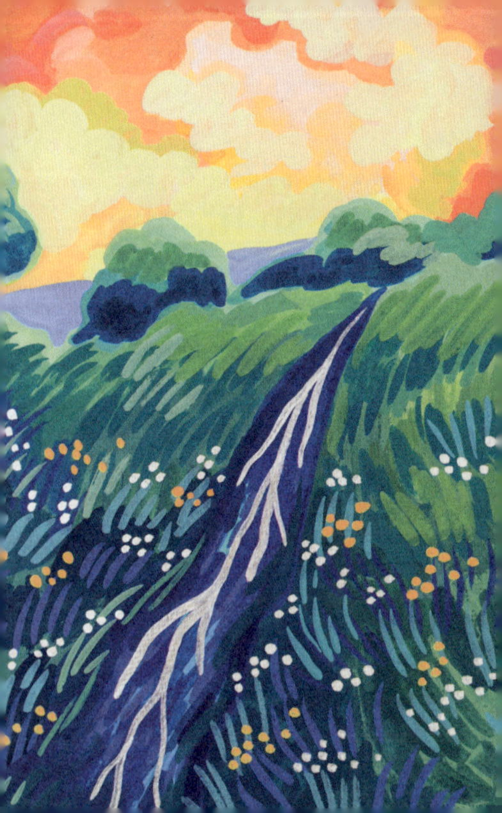

Repairing Relationships

Synopsis

This week's passage from Leviticus explores our need for healing and forgiveness in our relationships, calling us to rebuild a path to one another through empathy, understanding, and the mending of broken bonds.

Reading Plan

- ○ Day 1 / Leviticus 4–6
- ○ Day 2 / Ephesians 4–6
- ○ Day 3 / 1 Kings 14–18
- ○ Day 4 / Psalms 72–74
- ○ Day 5 / Proverbs 5–6
- ○ Day 6 / Ezekiel 7–12
- ○ Day 7 / Luke 13–14

Read—Leviticus 4–6

Leviticus 4–6 asks us to reckon with the messy reality of human relationships and the inevitability of causing harm—whether by accident, ignorance, or intention. Detailing the offerings and actions required by God to atone for various kinds of grievances, these passages make us mindful of the numerous ways in which we can hurt each other and the necessity of clear paths toward reconciliation.

In the complexity of the human condition, we fall short, both deliberately and inadvertently. Jesus reaffirms this reality in the Gospel of Luke, remarking on the universal human need for forgiveness.[1] Yet, Leviticus and Luke both demonstrate that no matter the grievance, there is a path forward—a path to restoration. The sacrifices of the Old Testament, with their specific circumstances and instructions, illustrate that making amends requires thoughtfulness, intentionality, and action.

[1] Luke 13:1-5, NIV

We must acknowledge what has gone wrong, accept our part in it, and work to set things right. This is easier said than done, but often we need to heal something in ourselves, perhaps something from our past, to heal in the present and for the future.

Interpersonal hurt and restoration can only happen within the context of our relationships with one another. Ephesians 4 tells us to think of our communities as living bodies.[2] Just as a body cannot function properly if one part is injured, a community cannot thrive if damaged relationships are left unaddressed. Every misdeed—whether intentional or accidental—is like a wound that needs to be treated to restore health. If the Leviticus passage provides instruction for how the Israelites were to address a grievance, Ephesians offers insight into how we can live in relationship with one another. "Get rid of all bitterness, rage, anger, harsh words, and slander, as well as all types of evil behavior. Instead, be kind to each other, tenderhearted, forgiving one another, just as God through Christ has forgiven you."[3] These practices are essential for a community in which all members flourish.[4]

Authentic relationship repair isn't one-sided, and it isn't a single event. It is a process that requires both repentance from the wrongdoer and forgiveness from the wronged. This mutual effort is vital for working through grievances and healing injuries toward a shared future. Laboring together to repair our relationships calls us into interconnectedness, our symbiotic thriving.

As Martin Luther King Jr. reminds us, "Whatever affects one directly, affects all indirectly [...] I can never be what I ought to be until you are what you ought to be. And you can never be what you ought to be until I am what I ought to be—this is the interrelated structure of reality."[5] Connection underpins every aspect of our existence. When we nurture our connections, we invest in the health and resilience of our communi-

[2] Ephesians 4:15-16, NLT / [3] Ephesians 4:31-32, NLT / [4, 5] See Endnotes

ty. It's through these connections that we find strength, support, and the capacity to forgive and heal. The work of repairing relationships is continuous. This week, may we consider joining in the constant work of relationality around us—and participate in the restoration of our world. Amen.

Reflect

I. Reflect, without judgment, on a past instance where you caused someone pain. What specifically triggered your actions? How did they affect the other person, and what steps can you take to begin healing that relationship?

II. If you've been hurt, consider what steps you might take towards reconciliation. How has reflecting on the nature of the hurt enabled you to engage in meaningful discussions?

III. Who in your life can support you in repairing or healing from relationships, whether that means seeking closure or reconciliation?

God of relationship,
Help us nurture our love
for one another and
to strengthen and support
our community
Amen.

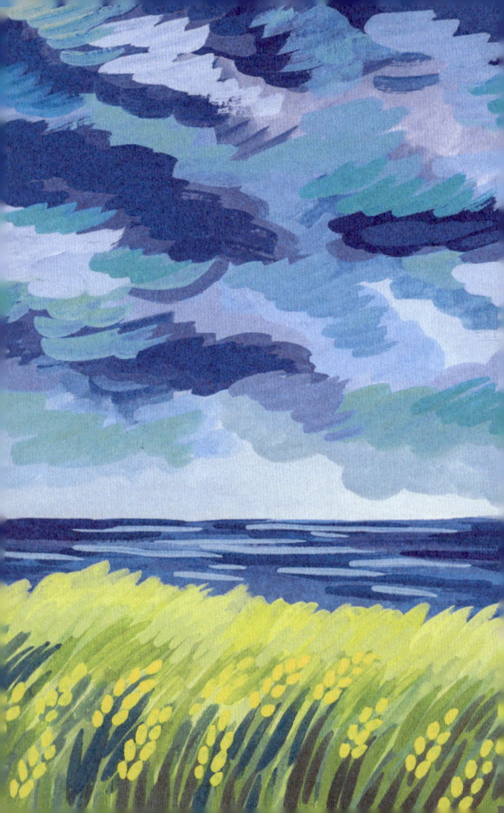

Finding God in Quietness

Synopsis

We learn to seek God's voice through quietness and solitude, amidst the distractions of our loud, noisy world through the example of Elijah's encounter with God in 1 Kings 19.

Reading Plan

- ○ Day 1 / 1 Kings 19–22
- ○ Day 2 / Philippians 1–2
- ○ Day 3 / Leviticus 7–9
- ○ Day 4 / Psalms 75–77
- ○ Day 5 / Proverbs 7
- ○ Day 6 / Ezekiel 13–18
- ○ Day 7 / Luke 15–16

Read— 1 Kings 19–22

In the rugged terrain of Mount Sinai, Elijah seeks refuge in a cave, exhausted after his intense confrontations with the prophets of Ba'al. His journey has been both physically and spiritually taxing, marked by miraculous victories and harrowing threats to his life. Amid this turmoil, God speaks to Elijah—not in the powerful wind that tears the mountains apart, not the earthquake that shakes the ground, or a fire that engulfs the landscape, but in a gentle whisper.

Life is loud, busy, chaotic. Often, we assume that the loudest voice in a crowd carries the most truth or influence. Yet, in contrast to our noisy world, God chooses to speak in whispers. This passage from 1 Kings assures us that this is indeed an intentional choice; God can command great winds and thundering quakes.[1] But in a gentle whisper, God appears

[1] 1 Kings 19:11-12, NLT

to Elijah with intimacy so contrary to the appearance at the altar of Ba'al. To hear a whisper, we must consciously quiet ourselves, draw near, and listen with intention. In a world that constantly pushes us to move faster and shout louder, God invites us to slow down, pause, and truly be present.

Waiting for God's hushed tones teaches us to be still and attentive, humbly waiting to be heard rather than talking over anyone else. This posture of humility reflects the gentle demeanor of Christ who, as Philippians 2 describes, humbled himself for our sake, embodying the strength found in surrender.[2] The quietness of God may seem subtle to us, but it holds immense transformative power like a persistent flow of running water, which over time carves canyons out of mountains. Theologian Henri Nouwen speaks to this idea—"It is in the faithful waiting for the loved one that we know how much he has filled our lives already."[3] What we often deem as weakness is laden with divine strength. Seemingly lowly states bring about universal salvation;[4] a single lost sheep is worth leaving the 99 to restore.[5]

Sometimes we become so busy asking God for answers that we forget to listen; we miss what God is saying to us gently. Psalm 77 reflects this tendency: "I cry out to God; yes, I shout. Oh, that God would listen to me!"[6] To be still and to search for God in quietness reorients us to the blessings and faithfulness God has shown us and reminds us that, no matter the circumstances, God's goodness and righteousness will have the final say. "But then I recall all you have done, O Lord; I remember your wonderful deeds [...] They are constantly in my thoughts. I cannot stop thinking about your mighty works."[7]

As we dive into these passages from scripture, let us challenge ourselves to embrace the quiet, to seek the whispers of God amidst our clamor-filled days. In doing so, we not only hear more clearly but deepen our relationship with the divine, finding God not only in the thunder but also in the tranquility.

[2] Philippians 2:5-8, NIV / [3] See Endnotes / [4] Philippians 2:9-11, NIV / [5] Luke 15:3-7, NLT / [6] Psalm 77:1, NLT / [7] Psalm 77:11-12, NLT

Reflect

I. Listening and quietude are virtues not often praised in our current day and age. In reflecting on these scriptures, how might you cultivate space to better listen for God?

II. Reflect on the passages of joyous salvation in Luke 15. How does practicing silence and solitude help you to better hear the voice of the searching shepherd?

II. Psalm 77 echoes the cries of many people longing to hear God but still waiting on an audible moment like Elijah. Recall the works of God as the psalmist does—in scripture, church history, and in your own life. How can these reflections serve as quiet encouragements in your life moving forward?

Mighty God of the whisper,
Thank you for guiding us back
when we stray from you.
You are our provider, giving us
sustenance like you did for Elijah.
May we see you at work and
hear your gentle voice.
Amen.

"

The quietness of God may seem subtle to us, but it holds immense transformative power like a

persistent
flow of running
water, which
over time carves
canyons out of
mountains.

”

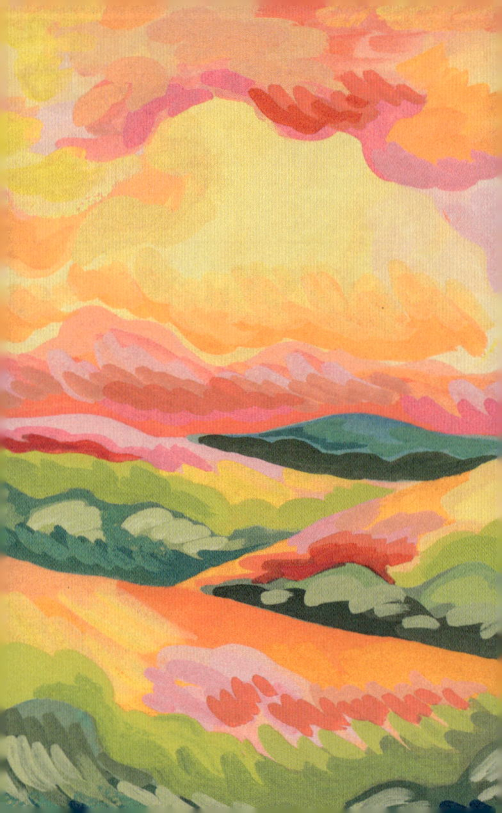

The Nature of God's Kingdom

Synopsis

God's Kingdom inverts our expectations and ushers in transformation. Luke 17–18 unpacks this notion, revealing how adopting a childlike posture of faith can open us to spiritual renewal.

Reading Plan

- ○ Day 1 / Luke 17–18
- ○ Day 2 / Philippians 3–4
- ○ Day 3 / Leviticus 10–12
- ○ Day 4 / 2 Kings 1–5
- ○ Day 5 / Psalms 78–80
- ○ Day 6 / Proverbs 8–9
- ○ Day 7 / Ezekiel 19–24

Read— Luke 17–18

In Luke 17, the Pharisees confront Jesus, asking when the Kingdom of God will arrive. To their surprise, Jesus upends the question, declaring that the Kingdom is already here.[1] Through a series of parables and teaching moments, he illustrates what the Kingdom of God truly looks and feels like. Jesus paints a compelling picture of a kingdom not defined by grand signs or future events but by the transformative presence of God's reign here and now.

Living into this kingdom means inverting our expectations. According to the world's standards, the best of us are self-assured and self-sufficient. Yet, in Luke 18, Jesus teaches that we must adopt a childlike posture—reliant and trusting upon God—to enter the Kingdom. "Let

[1] Luke 17:21, NLT

the children come to me, and do not hinder them, for the Kingdom of God belongs to such as these. Truly I tell you, anyone who will not receive the Kingdom of God like a little child will never enter it."[2] Children, with their innate trust and dependence on their parents, embody the humility and openness required to live in God's Kingdom. In other words, embracing a Kingdom mindset means acknowledging that we are not in control and submitting ourselves to God's guidance.

This posture can be challenging to adopt, standing in stark contrast to conventional notions of control and power. We often seek to manage our lives meticulously, striving to predict what lies ahead and adopting personal metrics for success. Psalm 78 speaks to this precise impulse, relaying a long history of humanity repeatedly choosing our own ways, over and above God's, to our detriment. When we rely on ourselves instead of relying on God, we miss the Kingdom of God being built in us and through us. The parable of the rich ruler likewise reflects the tension between human interests and divine instruction. Jesus emphasizes the difficulty the wealthy face in entering God's Kingdom due to their reliance on material wealth. Wealth and power are not inherently bad, but the illusion of control they can cultivate often makes it harder for us to turn to and fully depend on God. Paul underscores this in his letter to the Philippians, writing, "I once thought these things were valuable, but now I consider them worthless because of what Christ has done. Yes, everything else is worthless when compared with the infinite value of knowing Christ Jesus my Lord. For his sake I have discarded everything else, counting it all as garbage, so that I could gain Christ and become one with him."[3]

May we meditate on the radical nature of God's Kingdom as we study scripture this week. Are we striving to control every aspect of our lives, or are we looking to God for guidance? The invitation of Jesus moves us to let go of our illusions of control and open ourselves to the transformative power of the Kingdom here and now. Let us live in this King-

 [2] Luke 18:16-17, NLT / [3] Philippians 3:7-9, NLT

dom with humility, trust, and an open heart, knowing that God is guiding us every step of the way.

Reflect

I. In what ways might embracing a childlike reliance and trust gently shift your current views on control and independence?

II. Take a moment to reflect on Psalm 78. Where can you shift from relying on your own understanding to seeking God's guidance more fully?

III. Consider Philippians 3. How does recognizing the infinite value of knowing Christ Jesus guide you to reevaluate your priorities?

God of the present Kingdom,
Thank you for teaching us
childlike trust and humility.
May we let go of our
need for control, to fully experience
your presence here and now.
Amen.

"

Let the children come to me, & do not hinder them,

for the Kingdom of God belongs to such as these.
”

— LUKE 18:17

Freedom & Reconciliation in Christ

Synopsis

As Paul describes in Colossians 1–2, growth comes not from rigid doctrines but from living a life deeply rooted in Christ's teachings. This is the means of experiencing spiritual freedom.

Reading Plan

- ◯ Day 1 / Colossians 1–2
- ◯ Day 2 / Leviticus 13–15
- ◯ Day 3 / 2 Kings 6–10
- ◯ Day 4 / Psalms 81–83
- ◯ Day 5 / Proverbs 10
- ◯ Day 6 / Ezekiel 25–30
- ◯ Day 7 / Luke 19–20

Read— Colossians 1–2

In Colossians 1–2, Paul addresses the community at Colossae amidst a period of spiritual confusion. As the early Church continues to grow and mature, some have asserted alternative or supplemental doctrines, giving long lists of practices and regulations the people must adopt.[1] Against this backdrop of theological uncertainty, Paul's message is succinct and clear: all Christians need to do is follow Christ. Unlike other traditions or philosophies of life that are rigidly prescriptive or ritualistic, following Jesus simply means living our lives according to his teachings and doing our best to live by his example. When we draw closer to Jesus and get to know him better, we live better lives as a result. In the words of Colossians 2:6-7 (NLT), "And now, just as you accepted Christ Jesus as your Lord, you must continue to follow him. Let your roots grow down into him, and let your lives be built on him. Then your faith will grow strong in the truth you were taught, and you will overflow with thankfulness." In

[1] Colossians 2:8, NLT

many ways, this commandment is an incredible invitation into a freedom more liberating than we could ever imagine.

A life of faith is personal, transformative, and founded on the freedom that Christ offers. Where other philosophies prescribe specific actions undertaken for their own sake, living out of Jesus' example releases us from arbitrary metrics and invites us to adopt a posture of compassion and gratitude. For example, we strive to love our neighbors not merely to be perceived as holy, but because they are God's children, deserving of our love and help. Missionary, author, and speaker Elisabeth Elliot exemplified this posture in her own life. In her book, *Let Me Be A Woman*, she gives her readers this truth: "Freedom begins way back. It begins not with doing what you want but with doing what you ought—that is, with discipline."[2] Freedom is contingent upon obedience to God, not ourselves. It is made possible by the reconciliation Jesus offer to us. The fruit of following Christ is a deeply fulfilled life.

Through Jesus, we find freedom from the impossible standards that can dominate our lives. As women in a heavily demanding world, we can easily become overwhelmed by never-ending expectations set up only to make us fail and feel like lesser versions of ourselves. But living up to this pressure is never what God asked of us. We are not ruled by our imperfections but reconciled through Jesus' perfection and our reliance on him. Consider Zacchaeus in Luke 19, a tax collector who is far from perfect. To those around him, Zacchaeus' mistakes and shortcomings define and discount him. Yet, Jesus blesses him, as Zacchaeus goes to great lengths to change his behavior after the example set by Jesus. He listens and obeys because he too wants to follow God, and in that, he is deeply blessed. Jesus is ultimately Zacchaeus' path to reconciliation.

God doesn't want us to buckle under the weight of perfectionistic standards, but to live freely: This is our God, the One who wants to lift the burdens from us so that we might walk in obedience in a weightless, lib-

 [2] See Endnotes

erating way. As we reflect on these teachings, let us strive to look beyond the rituals and checkboxes. May we seek to live every day in the footsteps of Jesus and embody the freedom Christ offers us.

Reflect

I. Consider Colossians 1–2. How does living according to Jesus' teachings offer a more liberating form of freedom compared to rigidly prescriptive philosophies?

II. How does the notion of true freedom involving discipline and obedience to God impact our daily lives?

III. Reflect on Zacchaeus' transformation in Luke 19. How can following Jesus' example lead us to reconciliation and freedom from the burdens of perfectionism?

Liberating God,
Thank you for your gift of freedom.
As we build our lives on the
foundation of your words,
may we draw closer to you.
Show us how to live freely in you.
Amen.

“We are not ruled by our imperfections but reconciled

through Jesus' perfection and our reliance on him.
”

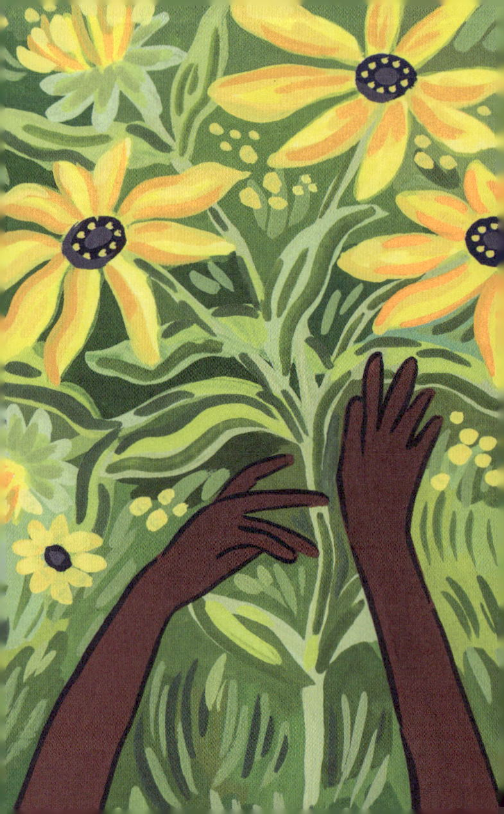

Divine Justice in an Unjust World

Synopsis

In Ezekiel, we explore God's vision of justice—one not rooted in retribution but in restoration. This vision calls us to pursue a world aligned with the biblical value of Shalom.

Reading Plan

- ○ Day 1 / Ezekiel 31–36
- ○ Day 2 / Colossians 3–4
- ○ Day 3 / Leviticus 16–18
- ○ Day 4 / 2 Kings 11–15
- ○ Day 5 / Psalms 84–86
- ○ Day 6 / Proverbs 11–12
- ○ Day 7 / Luke 21–22

Read—Ezekiel 31–36

What do we mean when we speak of justice? It's a concept often framed in terms of retribution and fairness—a "balancing of scales." Is it a universal truth or an outcome we must enact? Justice is something everyone seems to desire, yet our understandings of it vary greatly. For some, it means ensuring wrongdoers face penalties or consequences for their actions. To others, justice is a means of protecting rights and distributing resources fairly. However, there is one thing on which we can agree: we live in a world in which injustice seems abundant. Amidst an unjust world, we wonder how God defines "justice."

In Ezekiel, God presents a vision of justice that is restorative, not retributive.[1] God longs for all to repent and be forgiven—even those we view as wicked. Psalm 85 affirms this: "You forgave the iniquity of your people and covered all their sins. You set aside all your wrath and

[1] Ezekiel 33:10-20, NLT

turned from your fierce anger."[2] We may bristle at such a picture. As author Jessica Nicholas explains, "Western views of justice are primarily focused on how things should be done—laws, rules, and what should happen when laws are broken. In Hebrew thought, justice is focused on what life should be like."[3] Justice is not a balance sheet on which enough "good" cancel out the "bad." Rather, what matter are the intentions of our hearts. Are we actively pursuing good? When we make a mistake, do we work to make it right? "Your people are saying, 'The Lord isn't doing what's right,' but it is they who are not doing what's right. For again I say, when righteous people turn away from their righteous behavior and turn to evil, they will die. But if wicked people turn from their wickedness and do what is just and right, they will live."[4]

God's justice is about bringing creation back into tune. Those who were abandoned are found and nourished. Those who did wrong are corrected and given the chance to learn from their mistakes. It is not about us "earning" a reward or restoration—redemption is offered for God's glory and the good of the world.[5] Justice is the means through which God moves us all back toward Shalom.

This understanding contrasts sharply with the performative "justice" enacted by the religious council in Luke 22. As the council members question Jesus, their aim is self-serving and punishment-oriented. They view Jesus as a problem to be removed and see "justice" as the name under which they can get their way. We recognize this kind of behavior all too well. We are angered and grieved by institutions and individuals who seem more interested in self-preservation and maintaining the status quo than in doing what is right. Scripture confirms that these things also outrage God.[6] We are reminded that the restoration of divine justice will have the final say. While worldly leaders may mislead or abandon their people, God intervenes and makes things right. "I will search for my lost ones who strayed away, and I will bring them safely

[2] Psalm 85:2-3, NIV / [3] See Endnotes / [4] Ezekiel 33:17-19, NLT / [5] Ezekiel 36:32-36, NLT / [6] Ezekiel 34:7-10, NLT

home again. I will bandage the injured and strengthen the weak [...] I will feed them, yes—feed them justice!"[7]

As we reflect on these passages, let us strive to align ourselves with God's justice, seeking restoration and equity in our world. Let us lift up our voices to champion the divine vision for creation defined by peace, reconciliation, and care.

Reflect

I. How does the concept of restorative justice presented in Ezekiel compare with your own views on justice?

II. Reflect on the words of Psalm 85. How do you react to the notion of God's desire for all to be forgiven and restored?

III. Consider the contrast between divine justice and the performative justice in Luke 22. How can we align our actions with God's vision of justice?

God of Justice,
You work continually to
restore us and bring
all of creation back into tune.
May we open ourselves to
your vision of justice and
join in with its unfolding.
Amen.

[7] Ezekiel 34:16 , NLT

"

God's justice
is about bringing
creation back
into tune.
Justice is the

means through
which God
moves us all
back toward
Shalom.

”

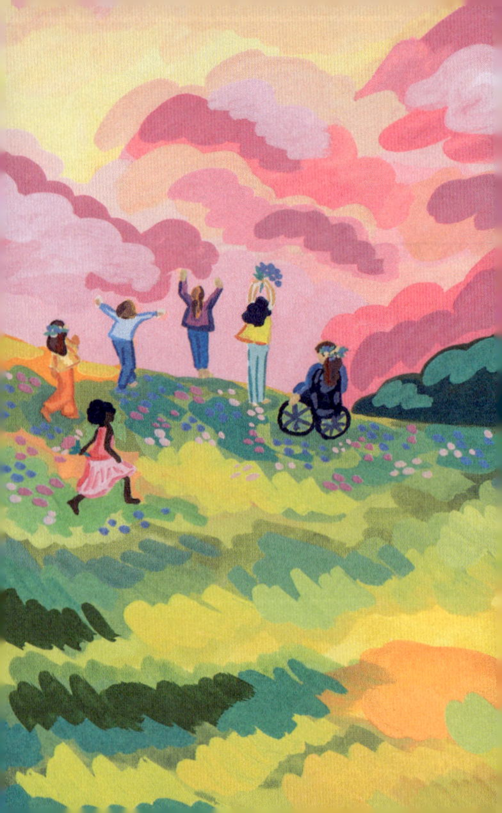

WEEK 30

Community of Believers

Synopsis

Through the relationship between Paul and the Thessalonians, we see an example of ideal community—marked by mutual care, fervent support, and embodying Christ's love.

Reading Plan

- ○ Day 1 / 1 Thessalonians 1-3
- ○ Day 2 / Leviticus 19-21
- ○ Day 3 / 2 Kings 16-20
- ○ Day 4 / Psalms 87-89
- ○ Day 5 / Proverbs 13
- ○ Day 6 / Ezekiel 37-42
- ○ Day 7 / Luke 23-24

Read—1 Thessalonians 1-3

Community is a fundamental aspect of human life. We all belong to various communities—neighborhoods, workplaces, and groups—and these connections shape our experiences. At its best, community offers belonging, support, and shared purpose. At its worst, it can be a source of exclusion, conflict, or competition, leaving some feeling unwanted or unheard. How do we look after one another? What does a truly supportive community look like?

In 1 Thessalonians 1–3, we find a vibrant portrait of a thriving community of believers. Through Paul's account of his time in Thessalonica, we see that living in community is about extending care and support to one another. Paul's relationship with the Thessalonians is marked by fervent prayer, diligent teaching, and constant encouragement, much like parents' guidance and intimacy with their children. In turn, the Thessalonian community welcomes Paul and his companions with open arms, provides for their needs, and shares their resources generously. This mutual support and genuine care reflect an ideal community where everyone looks out for one another, much like a family. Here, we see a beautiful picture of believers living in harmony, supporting one another, and embodying the love and care of Christ.

Community is also a means to uplift one another. When we dwell in unity, no one needs to bear burdens alone. Instead of focusing on individual needs, the community prioritizes collective strength and support. Leviticus 19 outlines how God desires us to treat each other, focusing on provisions for fairness, forgiveness, and love. It instructs us not to put ourselves over our neighbor but to foster a community where everyone is valued and cared for.[1] True community thrives on this collective support and mutual respect. As Archbishop Desmond Tutu declared, "I am human because you are human. My humanity is caught up in yours."[2]

Above all, an ideal community is for everyone. Psalm 87:5-6 celebrates this vision of inclusivity, stating, "Regarding Jerusalem it will be said, 'Everyone enjoys the rights of citizenship there and the Most High will personally bless this city.' When the Lord registers the nations, he will say, 'They have all become citizens of Jerusalem.'" This notion echoes in the concept of "the beloved community" championed by Martin Luther King Jr., and his wife, Coretta Scott King, envisioning a society rooted in love and justice. As Coretta Scott King describes, "The Beloved Community is a state of heart and mind, a spirit of hope and goodwill that transcends all boundaries and barriers and embraces all creation."[3] This vision calls for a community where everyone is welcomed and valued, overcoming division and fostering unity.

This week's readings challenge us to consider how we care for one another. Scripture calls us to build communities that are generous, mutual, and inclusive, focusing on collective strength and support while welcom-

 [1] Leviticus 19:9-18, ESV / [2,3] See Endnotes

ing and valuing everyone. As we strive to build such communities, we reflect the divine ideal of a harmonious, caring family of believers living out the principles of fairness and kindness that God has laid out for us.

Reflect

I. What does community mean to you? How have you experienced community in your life?

II. How can you extend care and support to those around you, just as Paul did with the Thessalonians?

III. What are some ways in which you can prioritize collective strength and support in your community?

Inclusive God,
Thank you for our communities.
Guide us to create safe,
supportive spaces where
all are valued and
goodness prevails.
Amen.

WEEK

31

Flourishing in God's Presence

Synopsis

We explore what it looks like to flourish by examining Ezekiel 43–48. In the picture of Israel's coming restoration comes the reminder that living according to God's guidance is the means to a nourished and fruitful life.

Reading Plan

- ○ Day 1 / Ezekiel 43-48
- ○ Day 2 / 1 Thessalonians 4-5
- ○ Day 3 / Leviticus 22-24
- ○ Day 4 / 2 Kings 21-25
- ○ Day 5 / Psalms 90-92
- ○ Day 6 / Proverbs 14-15
- ○ Day 7 / John 1-2

Read— Ezekiel 43-48

In Ezekiel 43–48, we dive deep into a detailed vision of the future restoration of the Temple and the re-establishment of worship rituals. This vision comes at a critical time for the people of Israel, who are living in exile. Ezekiel's vision echoes the instructions God first gave to Moses in Leviticus,[1] reminding the people of God's plan for their well-being. Now, as God gives Ezekiel a vision of Israel's restoration, these guidelines are laid out again, calling God's people to recommit themselves to God's ways of worship—because, in doing so, they will flourish.

Deeply rooted, spiritually nourished lives can withstand the tests of time and bear fruit for the long haul. As the psalmist explains, "The godly

[1] Leviticus 21–24, NIV

will flourish like palm trees and grow strong like the cedars of Lebanon. For they are transplanted to the Lord's own house. They flourish in the courts of our God. Even in old age they will still produce fruit; they will remain vital and green."[2] Just as palm trees and cedars are known for their longevity and sturdiness, so too will those who root themselves in God's nourishing presence thrive. These trees not only survive—they stand tall and resilient, roots deeply embedded in fertile soil, drawing sustenance that enables them to weather storms and droughts alike.

God desires the holistic, long-term flourishing of our whole world and every person and community in it. As Lisa Sharon Harper writes, "If we are human, then we are created to flourish and exercise agency in the world—economic and political, as well as social and cultural, agency."[3] Flourishing holds many dimensions; God invites us to partner in creativity and hope, courageously building a world where all can thrive.

With this bigger picture in view, we see that the instructions God gives us are not arbitrary. Rather, they are wise guidelines, written with our best interests in mind. As the psalmist reminds us, God is our refuge, near to those who need rescue.[4] God is trustworthy; we can choose to trust[5] God's ways of sharing unconditional love, courageous peacemaking, and a steady commitment to all people's flourishing. God is love, and God's commands teach us to love one another.[6]

Living in accordance with God's commands aligns us with the divine source of wisdom itself—the Holy Spirit. Abandoning this wisdom will inevitably lead us astray, cutting us off from that which nourishes us, like a tree without sunlight. Our spiritual connection with God enables us not only to survive but also to truly flourish.

As we reflect on this week's readings, let us consider our own foundations. Each day offers a new opportunity to deepen our roots in God's

[2] Psalm 92:12-14, NLT / [3] See Endnotes / [4] Psalm 91:2, 9-16, NLT / [5] Psalm 91:2, NLT / [6] 1 Thessalonians 4:9, NIV

teachings, building strength and fruitfulness in our lives. May we grow and thrive in the grace and truth of God's presence. Amen.

Reflect

I. What does it look like to simply be in God's nourishing presence? How can we take time to *be* and not *do*?

II. Where do you see the world around you needing nourishment from God's presence? How can we be the embodiment of God's presence to help bring about the flourishing of the world?

III. Are there areas of your life that need nourishment? How can you seek out God's presence and be rooted in Christ this week?

Nourishing God,
Thank you for always being
our safe place where
we can flourish.
May we help guide others to
your presence, and
bring about the
flourishing of our world.
Amen.

"

The godly will flourish like palm trees & grow strong like the cedars of Lebanon.

Even in old age they will still produce fruit; they will remain vital and green.

”

— PSALM 92:12, 14

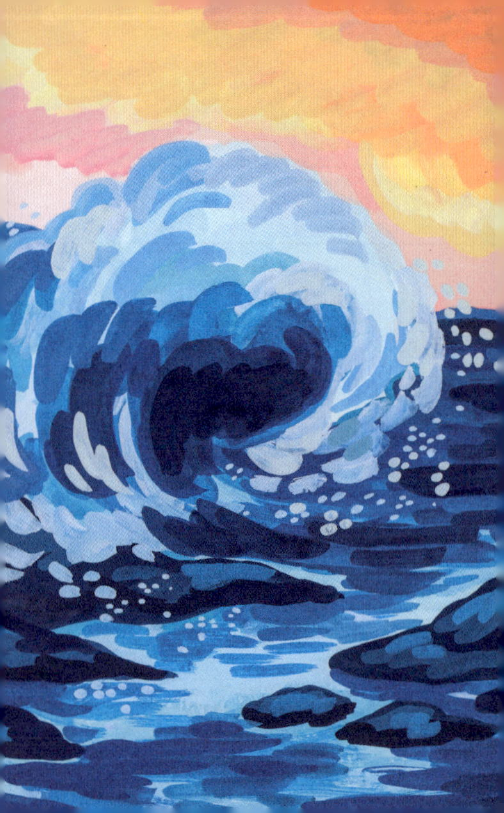

Strength & Perseverance

Synopsis

In 2 Thessalonians, Paul highlights how leaning into God in difficult seasons sustains us and leads to spiritual growth—affirming the power of God as our strength and anchor in times of turmoil.

Reading Plan

- ◯ Day 1 / 2 Thessalonians
- ◯ Day 2 / Leviticus 25–27
- ◯ Day 3 / 1 Chronicles 1–4
- ◯ Day 4 / Psalms 93–95
- ◯ Day 5 / Proverbs 16
- ◯ Day 6 / Daniel 1–6
- ◯ Day 7 / John 3–4

Read— 2 Thessalonians

As we journey through life, we inevitably face seasons of challenge and uncertainty. In these moments, we often feel pushed to our limits and wonder how we will navigate the difficulties ahead. In 2 Thessalonians, Paul addresses such seasons, assuring us that God strengthens us in times of trouble. Paul reiterates to the Thessalonians that their perseverance and faith amidst persecution will lead to their ultimate glorification. Holding fast to faith in difficult times isn't just about enduring hardship; it's about trusting that God will bless and sustain us through it all.

To be strong and perseverant means leaning on one another and depending on God. The wisdom and teachings given to us by God are our lifeline. In periods of crisis, leaning into God helps guide us safely through and encourages us to uplift each other.[1] By embracing our faith and the

[1] 2 Thessalonians 2:15, NIV

support of our community, we discover the resilience needed to persevere through life's challenges. Just as navigating an icy road requires leaning into the skid to regain control, so too can we find stability in times of trouble by leaning into our faith and the support of those around us. By doing so, we can stay the course and emerge stronger on the other side. This powerful combination of faith and community provides a steadfast anchor in the midst of turmoil, empowering us to weather any storm.

The story of Daniel exemplifies remarkable strength and perseverance in the face of adversity. Under foreign rule, Daniel, Shadrach, Meshach, and Abednego remain steadfast in their faith, defying immense challenges and dangers. Their unwavering trust in God empowers them to resist the pressures surrounding them, and God's protection and preservation are their reward. Daniel's steadfast faith is not some superpower—an ability he has that the rest of us lack. Rather, strength and perseverance are God-given. When we reach our limits, we can draw on God's limitless strength to carry us through. This divine dynamic is exemplified in Leviticus 25: "You may ask, 'What will we eat in the seventh year if we do not plant or harvest our crops?' I will send you such a blessing in the sixth year that the land will yield enough for three years."[2]

Paul also emphasizes that strength and perseverance are about not only surviving trials but also growing in faith through them. He writes, "May our Lord Jesus Christ himself and God our Father [...] encourage your hearts and strengthen you in every good deed and word."[3] By committing ourselves to God's guidance, we solidify our footing, and our perseverance bears fruit, transforming obstacles into catalysts for spiritual growth. As Proverbs 16:3 declares, "Commit your actions to the Lord, and your plans will succeed."

As we reflect on these readings from scripture, let us find courage in our faith and community. By entrusting ourselves to God's care and leaning on one another, we can confront even the most daunting challenges with

 [2] Leviticus 25:20-21, NIV / [3] 2 Thessalonians 2:16-17, NIV

resilience and emerge stronger, wiser, and more radiant. Let us lean into our faith, embracing God's guidance to help us navigate difficulty and lead us to a richer, more fulfilling life. Amen.

Reflect

I. What current challenges are you facing, and how can leaning on your faith and community help you navigate them?

II. Reflect on a time when you felt God's strength during a difficult period. How did that experience shape you?

III. In light of Proverbs 16:3, what does committing your actions to the Lord look like in your daily life?

God of Strength,
Through all of life's challenges,
you are there.
Fortify us with your might,
and guide us to lean
on our faith and community.
Amen.

"

Holding fast to faith in difficult times isn't just about enduring hardship; it's about trusting that God will bless and sustain us through it all. ”

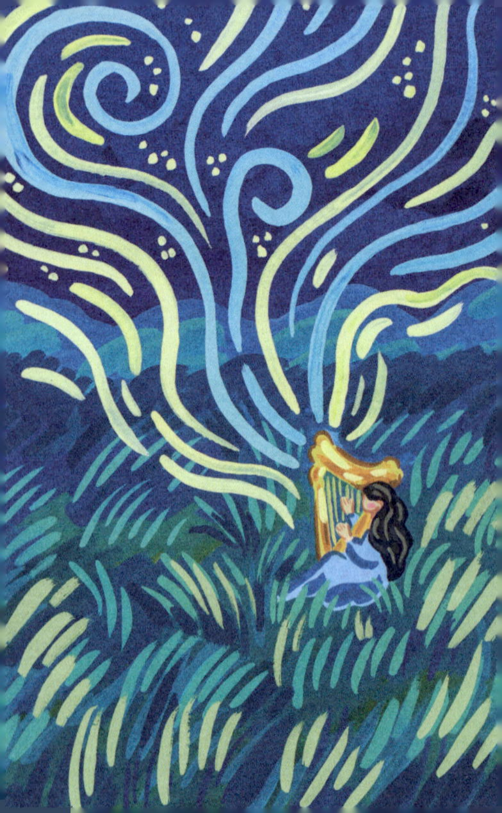

WEEK 33

The Joy of Worship

Synopsis

Worship springs from understanding God's immense power and grace. Rather than a task or obligation, this week's passages invite us to join creation's chorus in celebrating God's glory.

Reading Plan

- ◯ Day 1 / Psalms 96–98
- ◯ Day 2 / 1 Timothy 1–3
- ◯ Day 3 / Numbers 1–4
- ◯ Day 4 / 1 Chronicles 5–9
- ◯ Day 5 / Proverbs 17–18
- ◯ Day 6 / Daniel 7–12
- ◯ Day 7 / John 5–6

Read— Psalms 96–98

The term "worship" is often used in Christian communities. For many, the word might evoke images of congregational singing, fervent prayer, or a general display of enthusiastic adoration, but what does it genuinely mean to worship? Why is worship an essential expression of faith?

Scripture draws a sharp contrast between worship driven by fear or obligation, such as that offered to false gods and authoritarian rulers,[1] and worship in response to being in relationship with God. Worship naturally flows from recognizing who God is. As Psalm 96 declares, "For great is the Lord and most worthy of praise; he is to be feared above all gods. For all the gods of the nations are idols, but the Lord made the heavens. Splendor and majesty are before him; strength and glory are

[1] Daniel 7, NLT

in his sanctuary."[2] If we step back and reflect on the awesome power of God—as the Creator of all things, Sustainer of our lives, and Redeemer of our mistakes—we cannot help but shout with joy and praise. If we think of worship as breathing, then our expressions of joy are an exhalation after we are filled with grace.

The psalmist describes a natural world that is, likewise, bursting with praise. Every element of creation, from the vast heavens to the teeming sea and the whispering forests, is actively participating in worship.[3] We are invited to join the chorus with a call to worship that reaches anywhere and everywhere. The very beauty of creation is an expression of worship for the Creator who brought it into existence. When we witness the complexity and intricacy of nature, we glimpse God's handiwork.

Even beyond the wonders of nature, divine glory is evident as God makes the impossible possible. We see this divine power and care in the miracles of Jesus as he heals the afflicted, feeds thousands who are hungry, and walks on water. In these encounters, over and over again, witnesses respond through awe and worship,[4] and how could they do otherwise? To worship is to draw near to God and keep our eyes fixed on the Lord's faithful nature. Worship acknowledges where God is at work, blessing and shaping ourselves and others.

As we step into this week's reflections, may we find our own ways to join in the chorus of creation. Let us carry awe and gratitude into every corner of our lives. Let us turn each moment into an opportunity for worship and every breath into a prayer. Amen.

[2] Psalm 96:4-6, NIV / [3] Psalm 96: 11-13, NIV / [4] John 6:14, NLT

Reflect

I. Recall a recent moment when you felt joy in God's presence. How did you express this joy?

II. Consider Psalm 97:7 in light of today's visual culture. How do you interpret the significance of seeing and being seen as a believer?

II. With the diverse expressions of worship in creation, how can you explore and embrace new forms of worship in your own spiritual practice?

Lord worthy of worship,
May we joyfully recognize
your presence in our lives,
letting our worship flow
abundantly in praise of
your goodness.
Guide us in
fresh expressions of worship,
in all seasons.
Amen.

"

If we think of worship as breathing, then our expressions

of joy are an
exhalation after
we are filled
with grace.
”

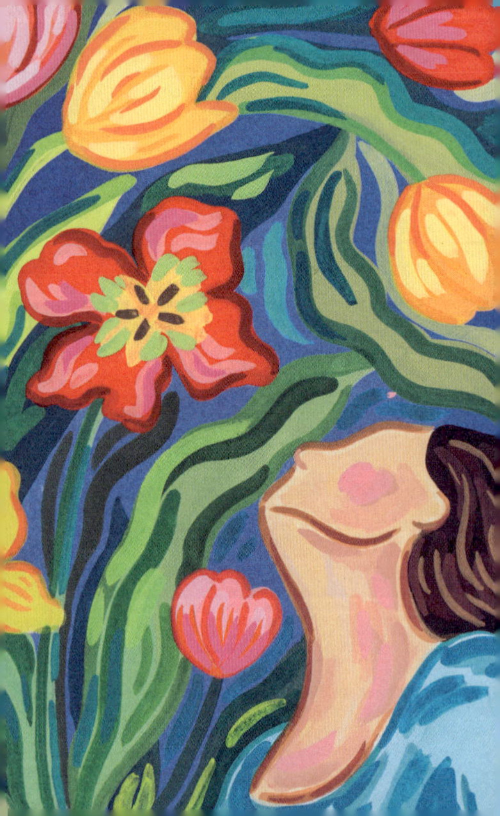

The Gift of Forgiveness

Synopsis

We reflect on the extraordinary gift of forgiveness through an exploration of John 8. Through this gift, we find a path forward, one marked by growth and reconciliation.

Reading Plan

- ○ Day 1 / John 7–9
- ○ Day 2 / 1 Timothy 4–6
- ○ Day 3 / Numbers 5–8
- ○ Day 4 / 1 Chronicles 10–14
- ○ Day 5 / Psalms 99–101
- ○ Day 6 / Proverbs 19
- ○ Day 7 / Hosea 1–7

Read— John 7–9

In John 8, in the dusty streets of Jerusalem, a dramatic scene unfolds. A woman caught in adultery is thrust before Jesus by the Pharisees, who are eager to test him. They try to use the situation to trap Jesus into both defying Mosaic law and clashing with the Romans. The Pharisees insist that the law demands the woman's condemnation, yet Jesus responds not with harsh words but with a quiet challenge: "Let any one of you who is without sin be the first to throw a stone at her."[1] One by one, the accusers depart, leaving the woman alone with Jesus, who, despite being the only one without sin—chooses to forgive her.

This story serves as a profound reminder of our shared need for forgiveness. God's forgiveness releases this woman from the punishment that was required of her so that she can walk into the light of new begin-

[1] John 8:7, NIV

nings. While the Pharisees strive to create division, Jesus uses the opportunity to demonstrate humanity's common need for a savior. Psalm 100:3 tells us, "Acknowledge that the Lord is God! He made us, and we are his. We are his people, the sheep of his pasture."[2] The path we travel together is riddled with pitfalls and missteps—everyone stumbles. Judgment and correction can only rightly come from one above reproach, the Chief Shepherd guiding us all. Out of the perfect grace God shows us, we are invited to extend forgiveness also—to those who have wronged us, affected us, or even misled us. In extending this forgiveness, we acknowledge God's abundant mercy and live out of gratitude.[3]

It is important to understand, however, that forgiveness does not equate to an absence of accountability or consequences. Forgiving is not merely about overlooking faults; it is a call to "go and sin no more."[4] In response to the forgiveness we receive from God, we strive to do better. By acknowledging wrongdoing and making amends, we take essential steps for true healing and restoration. Numbers 5:5-9 demonstrates the intentionality and accountability that reconciliation requires of us. When a rupture occurs, it must be made right. Since we were forgiven while we were still sinners, we are moved to turn from the behavior that required forgiveness to begin with. In the light of forgiveness, we can lift our heads from the weight of vengeance, and experience the air of freedom in letting go.

Forgiveness, in its deepest sense, involves both recognizing the harm done and choosing a path forward that fosters reconciliation and growth. However, forgiveness can also occur independently from relational repair. It allows us to release anger and resentment, even if the one who wronged us has not sought our forgiveness or is no longer in our lives. The choice to forgive is an act of strength, not defeat. It frees us from the burden of ongoing bitterness and empowers us to live fully in the present, unchained from past grievances.

As we reflect on these teachings, let us consider what it looks like to for-

 [2] Psalm 100:3, NLT / [3] See Endnotes / [4] John 8:11, NIV

give ourselves and others. Let us ruminate on the gift that is Jesus' forgiveness, embracing it and sharing it with everyone we meet. May we live out the great mercy we've received, fostering peace and reconciliation in our daily interactions. Amen.

Reflect

I. How does Jesus' compassionate response in John 8 challenge your current understanding of forgiveness?

II. Consider the balance between forgiveness and accountability. How can you apply these principles to foster healing and restoration in your relationships this week?

III. How has giving or receiving forgiveness influenced your ability to live more fully in the present?

Forgiving God,
Because of you,
we have forgiveness.
Thank you for this abundant gift.
Help us embrace this endless
forgiveness you have given, and
extend this gift to those around us.
Amen.

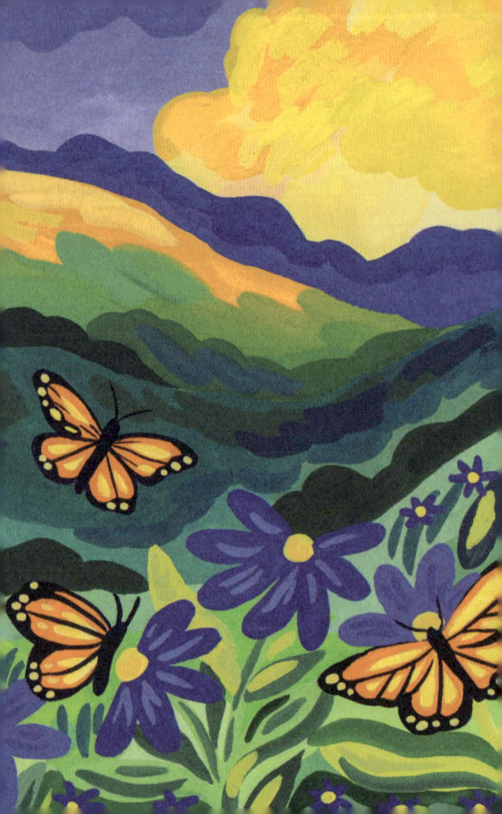

WEEK 35

Divine Callings

Synopsis

In our readings this week, we reflect on the diverse paths of God's callings and the challenges of embracing our unique roles in a world prone to comparison.

Reading Plan

- ○ Day 1 / 1 Chronicles 15–19
- ○ Day 2 / 2 Timothy 1–2
- ○ Day 3 / Numbers 9–12
- ○ Day 4 / Psalms 102–104
- ○ Day 5 / Proverbs 20–21
- ○ Day 6 / Hosea 8–14
- ○ Day 7 / John 10–12

Read—1 Chronicles 15–19

In 1 Chronicles, we witness the fulfillment of David's divine calling. A grand procession unfolds as he brings the Ark of the Covenant to Jerusalem. Musicians play harps and lyres, and David dances with all his heart. The streets echo with celebration at this pivotal moment in Israel's history. Yet, in the shadows of this joyful display, David's wife, Michal—the daughter of David's predecessor, Saul—looks on in contempt. Her ire harkens back to the jealousy that characterized her father's reign.

Many of us experience the temptation to compare our own paths to the paths of others. Seeing others thrive in their ministries, careers, or personal lives can make us feel as though our own achievements are not enough. Like Saul did with David, we often feel as though other people's success threatens our own. Social media amplifies these feelings, cultivating a culture of competition and comparison. We might make assumptions about others' lives based on what we see, even though we know the whole picture is more complex than what curated profiles depict. We might wonder if we are making any impact. How do we live into our callings among one another?

God's callings often look vastly different for each of us. Recognizing the uniqueness of our callings can free us from our tendencies to compare and compete. We see this potential in David's story. Chosen by God from humble beginnings to be king of Israel, David's leadership would become legendary. But a time comes when David's heart is set on building a temple for God, and God tells him that this task will not be his—it is reserved for his son, Solomon.[1] David's calling is not all he had hoped. Sometimes our callings are not what we expected or dreamed of either. But every person's calling is crucial to the health of our communities, and no one's calling is more important than anyone else's. David's calling to lay the groundwork for Israel's stability allows Solomon to focus on building the Temple. Each role is essential.

Living into God's call is not about personal glory or status but about serving God and one another faithfully. Mindsets of comparison, jealousy, and personal ego distract us and prevent us from experiencing the opportunities God invites us into. In John 12, we're told that many of the religious leaders understand the truth about Jesus but choose not to follow him. "For they loved human praise more than the praise of God."[2] In Numbers 11, jealousy drives Joshua to try to impede the movement of God's Spirit among the people.[3] John the Baptist prepares the way for Jesus, seeking not his own recognition or glory but leading many to believe in Jesus.[4]

We find our callings by listening to God's voice stirring within us. We pay attention to the gifts God has given us; we look for creative ways to love God and others well and to sow seeds of peace and justice in our world. We know we're on good paths not because they're the same as someone else's—or because they're what other people expect of us—

[1] 1 Chronicles 17:1-12, NLT / [2] John 12:43, NLT /
 [3] Numbers 11:26-29, NIV / [4] John 10:40-42, NIV

but because we sense divine life in our paths. Our contributions are measured not by their visibility but by our faithfulness. We can serve joyfully, trusting in God's wisdom and timing. Let us participate uniquely in God's Kingdom work as our authentic selves. May we embrace our callings with joyful hearts, echoing David in his uninhibited songs of praise.

Reflect

I. Have you ever sensed that God was calling you to something unexpected or different from your current path? What did that feel like?

II. How has pursuing your own calling brought you closer to God?

III. How can we acknowledge and support the unique callings of others? What does it look like to collaborate effectively despite our differences?

God who calls us,
Help us hear your divine
appointments for our lives.
May we be grateful for the unique
paths you have for each of us, and
may we encourage one another
as we pursue the callings
you have for us all.
Amen.

WEEK 36

The Holy Spirit is Our Advocate

Synopsis

The Holy Spirit's role is our advocate guiding us towards a life of abundance. This advocate guides us forward along the path God has laid out for us.

Reading Plan

- ○ Day 1 / Joel
- ○ Day 2 / 2 Timothy 3–4
- ○ Day 3 / Numbers 13–16
- ○ Day 4 / 1 Chronicles 20–24
- ○ Day 5 / Psalms 105–107
- ○ Day 6 / Proverbs 22
- ○ Day 7 / John 13–15

Read—Joel

In the Book of Joel, we are presented with the devastating aftermath of a locust plague that has ravaged Israel, bringing with it famine and fear. Amid this chaos, the people of Israel have gone astray, and they are in dire need of guidance and deliverance. This picture of a community in crisis is one we can still relate to today. In a confusing and chaotic world, many will claim to have all the answers, beckoning us to forsake God's wisdom and instruction.[1] Thankfully, we have been given the gift of the Holy Spirit, a dependable advocate reminding us to seek divine help always.

When we deviate from God's ways, we find ourselves in a world of competition and scarcity. Anxiety and uncertainty abound, and selfishness prevails. We can quickly fall for lies suggesting that we are not good

[1] 2 Timothy 3:1-5, NIV

enough, smart enough, or strong enough to meet all the demands of the world. This bleak reality contrasts sharply with the vision of flourishing and restoration that God promises in Joel 2:18-27—a picture of the abundance and peace that awaits those who live faithfully. In this, the Holy Spirit serves as our advocate, actively making a way for us when we are vulnerable, weak, or unable to see clearly. The promise of the Spirit is one of transformation, enlightenment, and a bold imagination for a new way forward. Joel 2:28-29 (NIV) prophesies as follows: "And afterward, I will pour out my Spirit on all people. Your sons and daughters will prophesy, your old men will dream dreams, your young men will see visions. Even on my servants, both men and women, I will pour out my Spirit in those days." To receive the Holy Spirit is to receive understanding; it is an invitation to experience God's vision for the world and live our lives in pursuit of that vision.

Jesus himself echoes this promise when he speaks of the Holy Spirit as an enduring presence in John 14:16-17 (NLT): "And I will ask the Father, and he will give you another Advocate, who will never leave you. He is the Holy Spirit, who leads into all truth." The Holy Spirit acts like a guide, keeping our eyes fixed on the path God has laid out for us and intervening when the trail feels unsteady. In the face of uncertainty, we can look to the Spirit to ensure that our choices align with love, mercy, and humility. When we stumble and go astray, the Holy Spirit is there to point us back to the center. As John 14:26 (NLT) reminds us, "But when the Father sends the Advocate as my representative—that is, the Holy Spirit—he will teach you everything and will remind you of everything I have told you."

This week, may we open ourselves to the Spirit, seek wisdom, and find guidance toward the abundant life God intends for us. May we lean into our divine advocate, who helps us discern wisdom from folly and keeps us grounded in God's will and power. Amen.

Reflect

I. Have you been actively living life in pursuit of God's vision for you and the world? What can you do this week to more fully invite that plan into your journey?

II. To embrace an advocate is to recognize that you need help. What is your immediate reaction or impulse when you can't do something on your own? Do you find this situation easy, or do you struggle to call out for help when you need it?

III. In what areas of your life do you need to let the Holy Spirit intercede?

Our Holy Advocate,
We are undoubtedly in need
in these times of trouble,
suffering, and inequity.
Would we rely on your Spirit to
intercede on our behalf.
For only you are wise and
just enough to guide us
through this world of strife.
Amen.

“

But when the Father sends the Advocate as my representative—that is, the Holy Spirit—

he will teach
you everything
and will
remind you of
everything I
have told you.
”

— JOHN 14:26

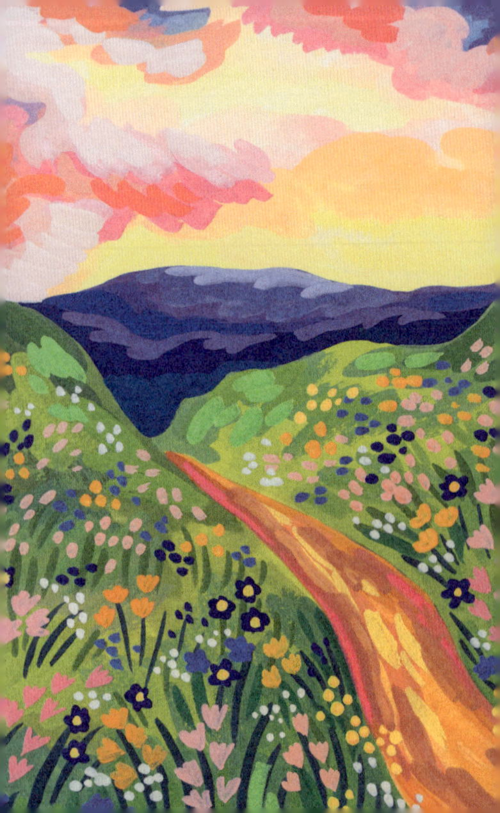

Leading Well

Synopsis

We explore a definition of leadership that advocates for humility, integrity, and service over authority and control. We are invited to embrace and navigate both the joy and responsibilities of a life of leadership that embodies the values of our faith.

Reading Plan

- ○ Day 1 / Titus
- ○ Day 2 / Numbers 17–20
- ○ Day 3 / 1 Chronicles 25–29
- ○ Day 4 / Psalms 108–110
- ○ Day 5 / Proverbs 23–24
- ○ Day 6 / Amos 1–4
- ○ Day 7 / John 16–18

Read—Titus

In the Book of Titus, Paul offers guidance to a young leader on what it means to lead well. For many, leadership evokes images of authority and control. We often admire leaders who are decisive, charismatic, and seemingly infallible. However, Paul presents a different notion of leadership in his letter to Titus—one that emphasizes humility, integrity, and service.

For Paul, good leaders lead by example: "And you yourself," he writes, "must be an example to them by doing good works of every kind. Let everything you do reflect the integrity and seriousness of your teaching. Teach the truth so that your teaching can't be criticized."[1] We are called to embody the values and principles we teach, inspiring others to follow suit.

Paul's invitation to live "a blameless life"[2] may sound unattainable, but perhaps we can also hear these words as humbling. We are fallible human beings, and even the best of us will not be blameless. Good leaders,

[1] Titus 2:7-8, NLT / [2] Titus 1:7, NLT

then, are quick to acknowledge their mistakes. They are not too proud to admit fault and make amends where possible. Healthy Christian leaders seek not their own glory but God's.

Throughout his life, Jesus exemplifies this kind of servant leadership. From healing lepers to facing criticism for spending time with tax collectors and sinners, to multiplying food to feed the masses, Jesus models what it looks like to lead with humility and love. His prayer in John 17 highlights his mission to help people know God and experience full, abundant lives.[3] When we follow Christ's example, we too become facilitators of this abundant life; we become connectors among people, building relationships marked by trust, honesty, and mutual encouragement. For Father Greg Boyle, this is a powerful vision of "Kinship—not serving the other, but being one with the other." Boyle continues, "Jesus was not 'a man for others'; he was one with them. There's a world of difference in that."[4]

Looking to Jesus as an example, we are called to build different kinds of leadership—and seek different kinds of leaders—than the models we often see around us. Dr. Brenda Salter McNeil draws a distinction between leaders "motivated by their xenophobic, competitive, and combative misuse of power for their own gain and self-aggrandizement," and leaders who operate with "collaborative, community-building power [...] power that works to counteract the divisive and destructive energy that is so pervasive in our world today."[5] Jesus embodied this community-building power.

The role of a leader carries gravity. It calls on us to be thoughtful and intentional, mindful that others will follow where we lead. In Numbers 18 the duties and regulations for priests are described as a "special privilege of service."[6] Leadership is a gift, a joyful call to partner with God in loving others.

God's call to leadership invites us into lives of humility, love, and a com-

[3] John 17:3-5, 12, NLT / [4,5] See Endnotes /
[6] Numbers 18:7, NLT

mitment to serve. Good leaders are not perfect, but they do aim to model the values they wish to see in their communities. In our daily lives, whether we lead in our families, workplaces, schools, neighborhoods, or churches, let us follow Jesus' example and lead with humility and integrity for the good of our communities.

Reflect

I. How does Paul's description of leadership in Titus influence your understanding of what it means to lead?

II. Reflect on Jesus' leadership style in the stories this week. How can you incorporate humility and collaboration into your own leadership roles?

III. Take a moment to be still and present with God. How might you feel called to take on a leadership role within your own community?

Lord,
Guide us to lead with
humility and integrity.
May we reflect your love
and serve our neighbors around us
just as Jesus did.
Amen.

"

When we follow Christ's example, we too become facilitators of this abundant life; we become connectors among people, building relationships marked by trust, honesty, & mutual encouragement.

”

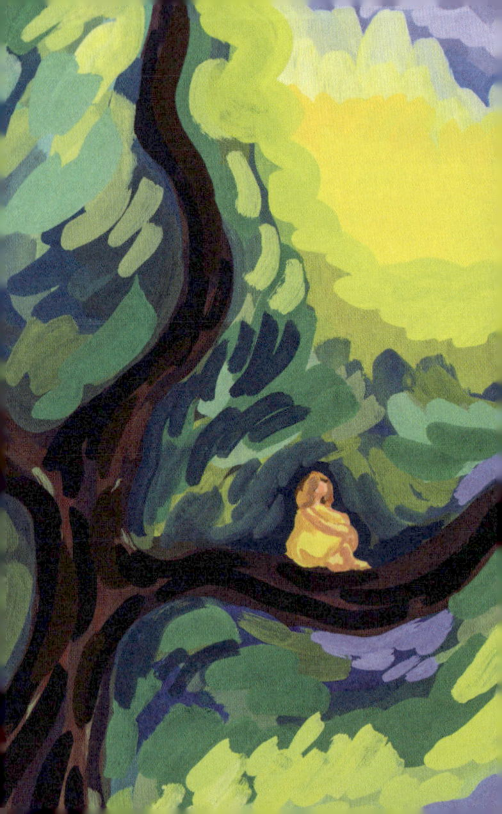

Work of the Cross

Synopsis

We explore the importance and purpose of Jesus' crucifixion and resurrection. Here, grace triumphs over condemnation and reconciliation over estrangement, showing us the God of fresh starts.

Reading Plan

- ◯ Day 1 / John 19–21
- ◯ Day 2 / Philemon
- ◯ Day 3 / Numbers 21–24
- ◯ Day 4 / 2 Chronicles 1–5
- ◯ Day 5 / Psalms 111–113
- ◯ Day 6 / Proverbs 25
- ◯ Day 7 / Amos 5–9

Read— John 19–21

The story of Jesus' death and resurrection is central to our faith. After an unjust arrest and the pretense of a trial, Jesus is crucified. The gathered crowd jeers, his mother bears witness in tears, and at the end of it all, Jesus dies and is buried. But then, three days later, when Mary Magdalene goes to the grave to pay her respects, she finds an empty tomb and Jesus himself very much alive. This is a very ubiquitous section of scripture, but what does it mean? Why do the crucifixion and resurrection matter so profoundly?

As we make our way through the Bible, a familiar pattern emerges time and again. God instructs humanity, clearly explaining the benefits of obedience and the consequences of disobedience. Nevertheless, humanity repeatedly chooses to go its own way, facing repercussions as God warned we would. While anger and frustration are a part of God's response to our disobedience it is also marked by profound sadness. The consequences that follow humanity's defiance come not from vindictiveness but as a part of the cause-and-effect nature of turning away from God. The vision of harsh judgment laid out in Amos 5–9 illustrates the grim fate that would be ours without the work of the Cross.

But thankfully, the biblical narrative does not end there, there is another repeated pattern. Time and again God mercifully intervenes to restore God's people. The work of the Cross and the Empty Tomb breaks the cycle of separation and return definitively, leaving grace and redemption as the final words. As Psalm 111 declares, "He has paid a full ransom for his people. He has guaranteed his covenant with them forever."[1] Jesus extends to us an eternal covenant, uniting us with God once and for all and clearing the slate of all the mistakes that came before.

John 21 depicts one of the very first acts Jesus undertakes following the resurrection and the moment serves as a profound illustration of the Cross's ultimate purpose. Following Jesus' arrest, Peter denied knowing him three times. By all rights, we might expect this decision to leave Peter irreparably separated from Jesus. But Jesus does not cast Peter aside; instead, he forgives and creates a path forward, drawing Peter into him.[2] This moment of healing is more than just a personal redemption for Peter but a clear demonstration of the new reality ushered in by the Cross—where grace prevails over condemnation, and reconciliation overcomes estrangement.

The story of Jesus reminds us that no failure is too great to be beyond the reach of God's redeeming love. Let us take a moment to consider how we might accept God's invitation to return and be restored, and how we can extend the same unconditional love and forgiveness to others around us. We give thanks for this divine model of restoration. It is the very heart of the Gospel, bringing us back into unity with our Creator. Amen.

 [1] Psalm 111:19, NLT / [2] John 21:15-19, NLT

Reflect

I. How does the story of Peter's restoration by Jesus in John 21 help you understand the depth of forgiveness available through Jesus?

II. Reflecting on Psalm 111:9, how does the concept of an eternal covenant of grace influence your approach to faith and daily life?

III. Consider the harsh judgments described in Amos 5–9. How does this passage make you feel? How might the grace and joy of John 20–21 help reframe the way you think about these Amos passages?

Lord Jesus,
Let us live in the freedom
and forgiveness of the Cross.
May we extend grace
as generously as
you have to us.
Amen.

"

The work of the Cross & the Empty Tomb breaks the cycle of separation

and return definitively, leaving grace & redemption as the final words.
”

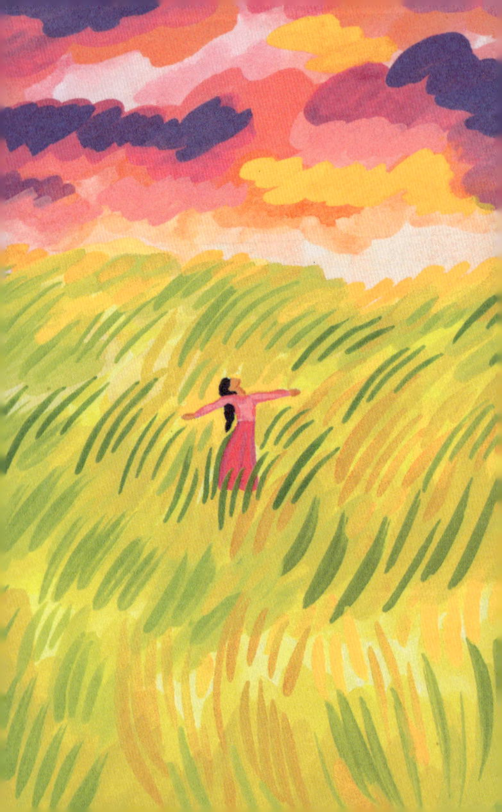

The Greatness of God

Synopsis

Psalms 114–116 highlights God's greatness, demonstrated not only through grand displays of cosmic power but also through an intimate presence among us.

Reading Plan

- ○ Day 1 / Psalms 114–116
- ○ Day 2 / Hebrews 1–4
- ○ Day 3 / Numbers 25–28
- ○ Day 4 / 2 Chronicles 6–10
- ○ Day 5 / Proverbs 26–27
- ○ Day 6 / Obadiah
- ○ Day 7 / Acts 1–2

Read—Psalms 114–116

When we talk of "greatness" we usually speak of being set apart, untouchable, and exalted. To be great is to achieve the extraordinary, wield unmatched power, and possess exceptional abilities. It draws to mind an athlete's unparalleled skill, a leader's profound influence, or a visionary's innovative brilliance. As we come to this week's readings, it is clear that God is great. Psalm 114 declares: "Tremble, earth, at the presence of the Lord, at the presence of the God of Jacob, who turned the rock into a pool, the hard rock into springs of water."[1] The Creator's power is expansive across all elements of our universe.

When we contemplate God through Psalms 114–116, we see divine greatness is immeasurably more. God is *above* us and, as the Creator

[1] Psalm 114:7-8, NIV

of all things, wields phenomenal cosmic power. Yet, God's greatness is not confined solely to divine power and majesty. It is equally expressed through God's desire to be intimately involved in our lives. God is *with* us. Psalm 116 describes: "The Lord is gracious and righteous; our God is full of compassion. The Lord protects the unwary; when I was brought low, he saved me."[2] God is not only omnipotent but also tenderly compassionate, eager to help us in our need.

The utmost supreme being will go to any lengths to be with us. Hebrews 2 points to Jesus as the ultimate expression of this: "Since the children have flesh and blood, he too shared in their humanity so that by his death he might break the power of him who holds the power of death [...] and free those who all their lives were held in slavery by their fear of death."[3] God is *among* us. Jesus embodies God's desire to dwell among humanity and is God's tangible expression of compassion and love. But Jesus is not the only example of God coming down to us. Scripture is full of demonstrations of God's desire to be with humanity, from the presence of God in the Temple[4] to the indwelling of the Holy Spirit during Pentecost.[5]

When approaching the greatest one of all, we assume they ought to be put on a pedestal, far out of our reach. However, what makes God truly great is that by all rights God could be set apart and yet God chooses to to identify with and live alongside us. "Let us then with confidence draw near to the throne of grace, that we may receive mercy and find grace to help in time of need."[6]

May we reflect on and celebrate the multifaceted nature of God's greatness. And may it enable us to deepen our relationship with the Creator.

[2] Psalm 116:5-6, NIV / [3] Hebrews 2:14-15, NIV /
 [4] 2 Chronicles 7, NLT / [5] Acts 2, NLT / [6] Hebrews 4:16, NIV

Reflect

I. What does God's greatness look like to you? How does Psalm 114's depiction of God's power over nature compare with your understanding of divine greatness?

II. Reflect on Hebrews 2:14-15 and the story of Jesus. In what ways does Jesus' life and sacrifice demonstrate God's willingness to engage intimately with humanity?

III. Consider the continual presence of the Holy Spirit in our lives. How does this shape your daily interaction with God?

God among us,
We marvel at your greatness,
not only in your mighty deeds
but in your compassionate closeness.
Thank you for dwelling
among us through Jesus.
May we be reminded every day of
your enduring love and grace.
Amen.

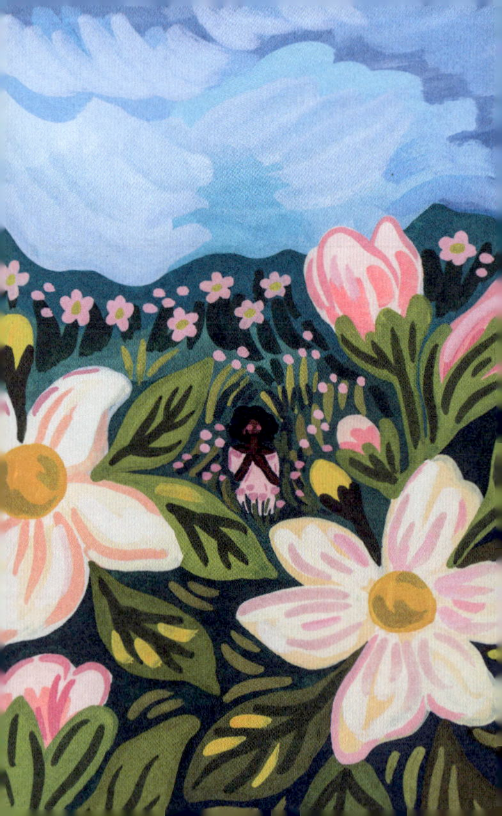

Compassion & Second Chances

Synopsis

Through the story of Jonah, we consider the power and challenges of extending second chances. We're all in need of grace and compassion, but forgiving those who hurt us can be difficult.

Reading Plan

- ○ Day 1 / Jonah
- ○ Day 2 / Hebrews 5–7
- ○ Day 3 / Numbers 29–32
- ○ Day 4 / 2 Chronicles 11–15
- ○ Day 5 / Psalms 117–118
- ○ Day 6 / Proverbs 28
- ○ Day 7 / Acts 3–4

Read—Jonah

When God commands Jonah to give the people of Nineveh a message of warning, Jonah's response is avoidance and disobedience. The people of Nineveh are his enemies and he wants no part in giving them a chance at redemption. Instead, Jonah turns his back on God, and the people of Nineveh, running in the opposite direction from where God directed him.[1] His defiance has consequences; the ship he's on finds itself caught in a mighty tempest and Jonah ends up swallowed by a great fish. In the belly of the beast, he prays for deliverance and, after receiving a second chance, commits to going to Nineveh. However, when God spares the repentant city, Jonah becomes intensely angry. This raises a fundamental question: Why do we struggle with the idea of extending grace and forgiveness, especially to those we feel have wronged us?

It is no mystery that forgiveness is hard. When we're angry or when

[1] Jonah 1:3, NLT

we've been wronged, the idea of our transgressor getting a second chance can be unappealing. Just as Jonah bemoans God's grace and compassion for Nineveh,[2] sometimes we too relish the idea of our enemies receiving due punishment. But Jonah's story cautions against this impulse to dole out justice through the lens of our thirst for vengeance. If we celebrate and give thanks for God's compassion and mercy when it is extended to us, we must reckon with the idea that this same grace extends even to those we dislike and disapprove of. Ironically, the second chance Jonah believes Nineveh is unworthy of is precisely the kind of second chance God has bestowed upon Jonah. As author C.S. Lewis said, "To be a Christian means to forgive the inexcusable because God has forgiven the inexcusable in you."[3]

We're all in need of forgiveness, even the most righteous among us.[4] The vindictive instinct Jonah feels causes him to forget that everyone is created in the image of God. Jonah's anger is not just misplaced; it is a profound misunderstanding of divine grace. As Jonah mourns the death of a shade plant, God gently reminds him of the greater significance of caring for people: "Then the Lord said, 'You feel sorry about the plant, though you did nothing to put it there. It came quickly and died quickly. But Nineveh has more than 120,000 people living in spiritual darkness, not to mention all the animals. Shouldn't I feel sorry for such a great city?'"[5] God's love and compassion extend to every corner of the world. By shifting our focus from grievances to grace, we align ourselves with God's boundless compassion. In the words of Psalm 117 (NLT), "Praise the Lord, all you nations. Praise him, all you people of the earth. For his unfailing love for us is powerful; the Lord's faithfulness endures forever. Praise the Lord!"

The story of Jonah is an invitation for sobering reflection. Are we holding onto grudges and wishing ill upon others? What does it look like to truly forgive and extend grace? This week, let us embrace the

[2] Jonah 4:1-3, NLT / [3] See Endnotes / [4] Hebrews 5:1-3, NIV / [5] Jonah 4:10-11, NLT

call to embody the compassion and mercy of God. In doing so, we restore our relationships with one another and deepen our relationship with God.

Reflect

I. Reflect on a time when forgiving someone was particularly challenging. Are there recurring patterns or specific individuals that consistently test your ability to forgive?

II. In considering Jonah's reluctance to see Nineveh forgiven, what personal biases might you have that hinder your ability to extend grace to others? How can you confront those biases?

III. Reflect on a time when someone extended you a second chance. How did that experience make you feel? How might that experience inspire you the next time you are in a position to offer grace?

Lord,
Teach us to forgive
as freely as you have forgiven us.
May we embody your compassion
in all our relationships.
Amen.

"

We're all in need of forgiveness,

even the most righteous among us.

”

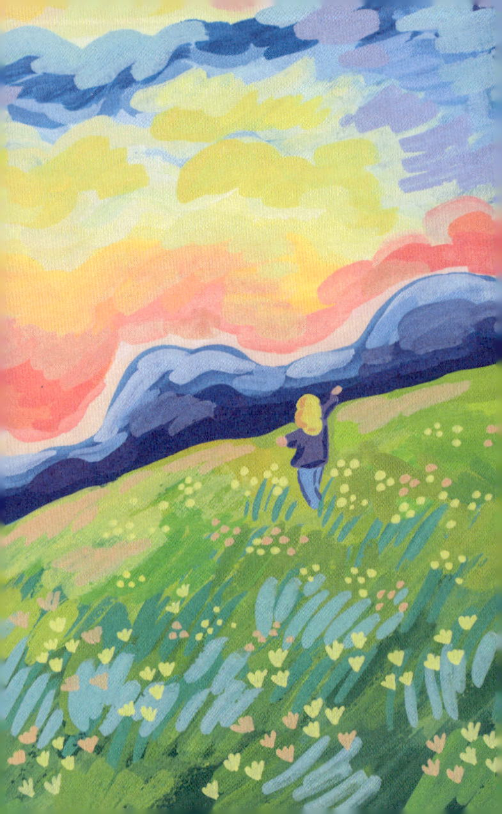

Jesus is Our Redeemer

WEEK
41

Synopsis

In this week's passage from Hebrews, we unpack the notion of Jesus as the ultimate redeemer—perfecting the ancient rituals by offering a new covenant that restores and continuously draws us closer to God's presence.

Reading Plan

- ○ Day 1 / Hebrews 8–10
- ○ Day 2 / Numbers 33–36
- ○ Day 3 / 2 Chronicles 16–20
- ○ Day 4 / Psalms 119
- ○ Day 5 / Proverbs 29–30
- ○ Day 6 / Micah
- ○ Day 7 / Acts 5–6

Read— Hebrews 8–10

This week's passage from Hebrews explores the idea of Jesus as our Redeemer. It's a phrase that is used often in faith circles—in sermons, studies, and hymns alike. But what does it mean exactly? As we read through scripture, we see God's longing to bring us back into a state of harmony and wholeness. Yet, when we look around, we see damaged relationships, the pursuit of personal gain, and the neglect of the needs of others. We try to get things right but fall short. Time and again, our Creator reaches out to us, calling us home and offering us means to leave our brokenness behind. Enter Jesus, the ultimate plan for our renewal.

Hebrews 8 explains, "Here is the main point: We have a High Priest who sat down in the place of honor beside the throne of the majestic God in heaven. There he ministers in the heavenly Tabernacle, the true place of worship that was built by the Lord and not by human hands."[1] In this, the author of Hebrews draws on the imagery and convention of Law given to Moses to demonstrate that Jesus is the perfect fulfillment of everything laid out in the Old Testament Law. Before Jesus, priests acted as he primary mediators between God and the people, offering sacrifices to atone for sins. The Tabernacle served as the sacred dwelling place of God among the people. This was the first model for humanity's redemption.

The purpose of all these systems—the priesthood, the Tabernacle, and the ritual sacrifices—was to make us right with God. They were designed to provide a way for humanity to atone for our sins and maintain relationship with God. However, no matter how hard we try, we remain imperfect. The Psalms reflect this frustration: "Help me abandon my shameful ways; for your regulations are good. I long to obey your commandments! Renew my life with your goodness."[2] Likewise, the old systems themselves had limitations by virtue of the fallible humans operating within them. The priests were imperfect. Sacrifices needed to be offered daily. The Tabernacle could only be entered by a select few. The institution and responsibilities of the priesthood, the Tabernacle, and the ritual sacrifices—all of these elements find their ultimate embodiment in Christ. "So Christ has now become the High Priest over all the good things that have come. He has entered that greater, more perfect Tabernacle in heaven, which was not made by human hands and is not part of this created world. With his own blood—not the blood of goats and calves—he entered the Most Holy Place once for all time and secured our redemption forever."[3] Through Jesus, we have a perfect way to be made right with God forever.[4]

How wonderful it is to worship a God of redemption and compassion! God draws us close, extends us abundant mercy, and delights in showing unfailing love.[5] In Jesus, we see the grand crescendo of a Redeemer who has been working for our salvation through all eternity. Jesus'

[1] Hebrews 8:1-2, NLT / [2] Psalm 119:39-40, NLT / [3] Hebrews 9:11-12, NLT / [4] Hebrews 9:25-26, NLT / [5] Micah 7:18-20, NLT

sacrifice invites us into a new covenant, one where our sins are forgiven and we are continually drawn closer to God. This week, as we engage with the scriptures, let us embrace the fullness of this redemption, recognizing the depth of Christ's sacrifice and the eternal hope it brings. Amen.

Reflect

I. Hebrews 8 describes Jesus as the High Priest. How does this role influence your understanding of his mediation between us and God?

II. Reflect on Psalm 119's call to abandon shameful ways and renew life with goodness. How does this resonate with your own journey?

III. Consider the transformative power of Jesus' profound sacrifice. In what ways can you more fully embrace his redemption in areas of your life where you see brokenness?

Jesus,
Help us embrace
your complete redemption,
seeing your perfect renewal
wherever there is brokenness.
Amen.

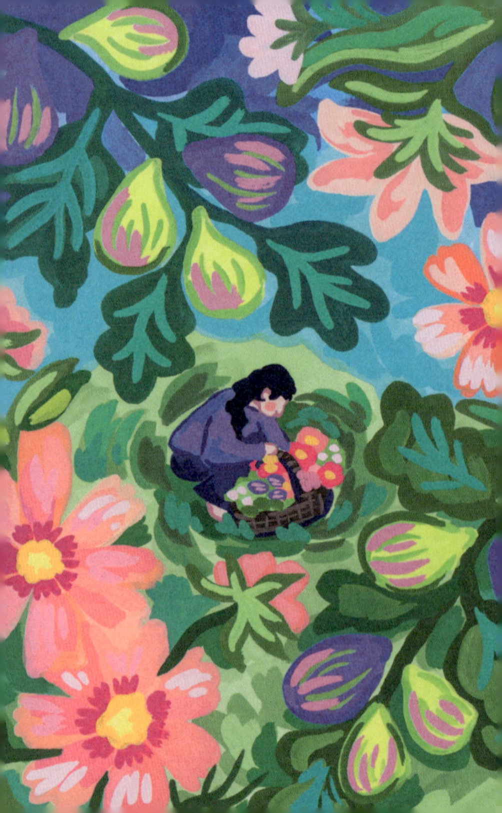

WEEK
42

Sharing Our Faith

Synopsis

We reflect on the importance of sharing our faith through the lens of Acts 7–8. The examples set by the early believers teach us what it looks like to extend the joyful gift of the Gospel to others with humility and love.

Reading Plan

- ◯ Day 1 / Acts 7-8
- ◯ Day 2 / Hebrews 11-13
- ◯ Day 3 / Deuteronomy 1-3
- ◯ Day 4 / 2 Chronicles 21-24
- ◯ Day 5 / Psalms 120-121
- ◯ Day 6 / Proverbs 31
- ◯ Day 7 / Nahum

Read— Acts 7-8

Throughout Acts, we witness the first believers preaching the Gospel throughout the world. Amid persecution, great geographic distance, and cultural differences, these early Christians persistently share their faith. These stories highlight the transformative power of faith and the impact it can have on people's lives. But what propels Stephen, Philip, and the other believers to share with others so fervently? What might it look like for us to follow in their footsteps and share our faith today?

Faith is powerful. It is the recognition of God's cosmic creativity[1] and the means through which we partner with God. When we live out of faith, we become instruments of God's transformative Kingdom. We see this when the author of Hebrews declares, "By faith these people overthrew kingdoms, ruled with justice, and received what God had promised

[1] Hebrews 11:3, NLT

them. They shut the mouths of lions, quenched the flames of fire, and escaped death by the edge of the sword. Their weakness was turned to strength. They became strong in battle and put whole armies to flight."[2]

At its core, to have faith is to trust God and live according to divine wisdom. Sharing our faith means inviting others to experience the beauty of God's plans too. Psalms 120 and 121 give us simple and joy-filled expressions of this, assuring us that God answers us in distress, and watches over and protects us.[3] There is a reason the gospel is called "good news." And once we have received such news, what can we do but pass it on? As evangelist and theologian D.T. Niles said, sharing our faith is like "one beggar telling another where to get food."[4] We share our faith because it has been so nourishing and life-giving for us.

In 2 Chronicles and the Book of Nahum, we see stark examples of the pain and suffering that can come when we try to go our own way apart from God. In this respect, sharing our faith is also a way of showing others a better way forward: one defined by love, not grief and fear. If having faith is like enjoying a banquet prepared by God, then sharing our faith is like inviting others to join the feast, so that they too can savor the richness and abundance of life with God.

Importantly, we are called to share our faith, not to impose it.[5] In Acts 8, Philip encounters a man struggling to make sense of scripture in his chariot. Philip reaches out in response to the Spirit's prompting, asking if he understands what he is reading. He asks a question first. The man then invites Philip to join him and explain the scriptures. Their conversation is deeply transformative, helping the man to understand the joy of the good news and leading him to faith.[6] A spirit of mutual respect characterizes the interaction. Philip does not make the traveling man feel inferior; he waits to be invited. Trying to force someone to listen to us and to accept Jesus is counter to the whole point of sharing our faith—we are extending a joyful gift, not issuing a demand.

[2] Hebrews 11:33-34, NLT / [3] Psalm 120:1, 121:5-8, NIV / [4, 5] See Endnotes / [6] Acts 8:30-36, NIV

This week, let us consider faith's power in our lives and how we can share it with others. As the Spirit leads, may we extend to others an invitation to experience God's love and restoration, embracing the opportunity with humility and love, so the whole earth can know of God's goodness.

Reflect

I. Take a moment to reflect on the people who initially shared the Gospel with you in meaningful ways. What was helpful about how they shared with you?

II. What are a few of the key aspects you find most compelling about your faith, and how do they influence your daily life?

III. Like Philip, do you sense the Holy Spirit prompting you to come alongside someone you have crossed paths with? How might you engage in a spirit of humility and mutual respect, waiting on God to open an opportunity to share about your faith?

God of Invitations,
Be with us as we share our faith with the world.
Let your Spirit be so palpable in us, that
others cannot help but invite us to share.
May we have a joyful and loving posture as
we live out of an abundance of faith,
enough to satisfy all.
Amen.

"

There is a reason the gospel is called "good news." And once

we have received such news, what can we do but pass it on?
”

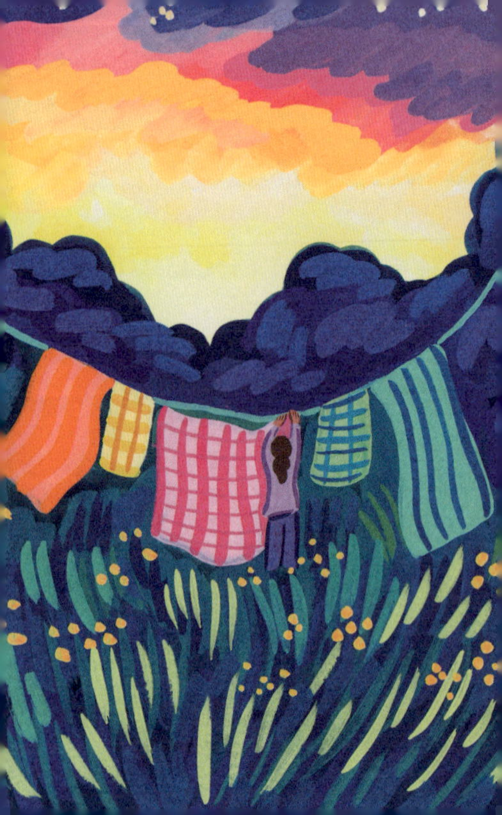

Living Out Our Faith

Synopsis

This week's passage from Deuteronomy urges us to embody faith as a driving force in our lives—transforming our belief into action by loving God and others.

Reading Plan

- ○ Day 1 / Deuteronomy 4-6
- ○ Day 2 / James 1-3
- ○ Day 3 / 2 Chronicles 25-28
- ○ Day 4 / Psalms 122-124
- ○ Day 5 / Ecclesiastes 1-2
- ○ Day 6 / Habakkuk
- ○ Day 7 / Acts 9-10

Read—Deuteronomy 4-6

Last week, we explored the concept of faith and the importance of sharing that faith with those around us. This week's passages invite us to dive even deeper into this idea. We know that faith is powerful and transformative, but what does it look like for faith to truly be the driving force of our lives? In answer to this question comes Deuteronomy 6:4-9, perhaps one of the most important passages of the Old Testament: "Hear, O Israel: The Lord our God, the Lord is one. Love the Lord your God with all your heart and with all your soul and with all your strength. These commandments that I give you today are to be on your hearts. Impress them on your children. Talk about them when you sit at home and when you walk along the road, when you lie down and when you get up. Tie them as symbols on your hands and bind them on your foreheads. Write them on the doorframes of your houses and on your gates."[1] Known commonly as "The Shema," this passage paints a picture of faith that is all-encompassing.

[1] Deuteronomy 6:4-9, NIV

Deuteronomy outlines the importance of remaining faithful and living our lives as God desires. More than a concept to be understood, faith is a way of life to be embodied in every action and thought. The reassertion of the 10 Commandments in Deuteronomy 5 demonstrates that faith is not just an idea or philosophy but an active, moving force. Our faith should drive us to do things (to love God, to honor our parents, etc.) and should guide us in what things ought not to be done (lying, theft, harming others). James 1 echoes this idea: "But don't just listen to God's word. You must do what it says. Otherwise, you are only fooling yourselves."[2] The way we live our lives should be a reflection of God's wisdom.

Think of a student learning a new language. She might learn all the vocabulary terms and study hard to pass the tests. But, there is a difference between learning theory and being able to apply it. If our student never utilizes her knowledge and cannot actually communicate in her new language, did she really learn it? Likewise, we must take the lessons of faith God shares with us and apply them to our daily lives.

Fortunately, scripture also offers us a clear picture of what life lived out of faith looks like: to love God with our entire being means loving and caring for others.[3] Acts 10 provides an example in the person of Cornelius. Cornelius is a man of great faith, demonstrated by his love of God and care for others.[4] Initially, Peter rejects Cornelius because he is a Gentile. He puts the traditions of faith over and above the righteousness of this person. But God recognizes the fruit of Cornelius' faith and welcomes him. "What good is it, dear brothers and sisters, if you say you have faith but don't show it by your actions?" James writes. "Suppose you see a brother or sister who has no food or clothing, and you say, 'Good-bye and have a good day; stay warm and eat well'—but then you don't give that person any food or clothing. What good does that do? So you see, faith by itself isn't enough. Unless it produces good deeds, it is dead and useless."[5] A life of faith ought to bear fruit.

[2] James 1:22, NLT / [3] James 1:27 / [4] Acts 10:2, NIV / [5] James 2:14-17, NLT

As we meditate on these passages, let us take the wisdom of the Shema to heart. Are we merely reflecting on our faith, or are we actively applying it in our deeds? Let us strive to embody a faith that is dynamic and transformative, one that drives us to love and serve others genuinely.

Reflect

I. Are there ways in which your faith is siloed into certain sections of your life, instead of being the all-encompassing faith laid out in the Shema?

II. How can we practice our faith in ways that transform the world around us and bear fruit that ultimately benefits ourselves and others?

III. What are some barriers that might keep your faith internal, residing only within your own mind and heart? How can you push past those barriers to lead a life of faith clearly evident to those around you?

Lord Our God,
May we love you with all
we have and all we are.
May our faith encompass all in our lives,
bearing fruit that blesses those around us,
and may our faithful hearts lead us to
action that reflects your love and wisdom.
Amen.

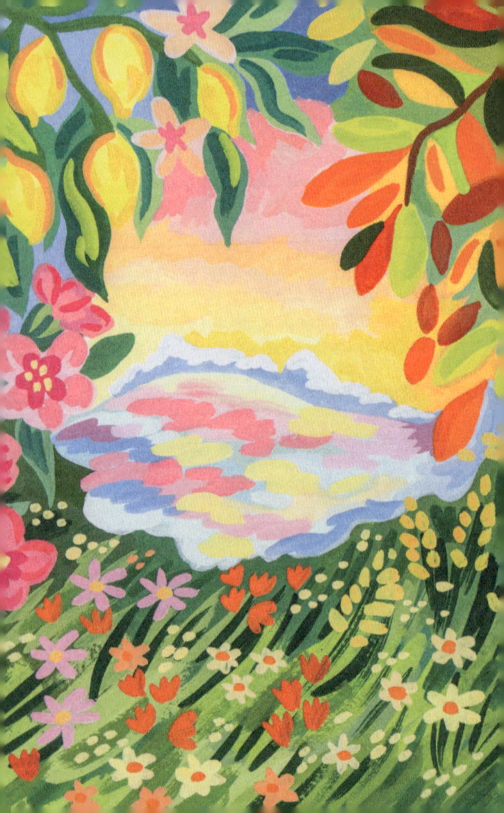

WEEK
44

Embracing Life's Seasons

Synopsis

In a constantly changing world, Ecclesiastes advises us to root ourselves in God's eternal wisdom rather than in fleeting institutions or our own strength.

Reading Plan

- ○ Day 1 / Ecclesiastes 3–4
- ○ Day 2 / James 4–5
- ○ Day 3 / Deuteronomy 7–9
- ○ Day 4 / 2 Chronicles 29–32
- ○ Day 5 / Psalms 125–127
- ○ Day 6 / Zephaniah
- ○ Day 7 / Acts 11–12

Read— Ecclesiastes 3–4

The longer we live, the more we experience life's ups and downs. Sometimes we may feel that the only predictable thing about our lives is unpredictability. One day we find ourselves basking in the warmth of fulfillment, and the next, grappling with unexpected hardships. Such ebbs and flows can be uncomfortable; we crave stability and meaning. And yet, as the Book of Ecclesiastes reminds us, these rhythms are natural. "For everything there is a season," the wise Teacher writes, "a time for every activity under heaven."[1] Change is inevitable, yet it can often leave us feeling disoriented or adrift.

In our search for solid ground, we might instinctively look to our established institutions, to political figures who promise security, or to the shared common wisdom of our culture. South African Anglican archbishop Desmond Tutu ruminates on this impulse: "In times such as our own—times

[1] Ecclesiastes 3:1, NLT

of change when many familiar landmarks have shifted or disappeared—people are bewildered; they hanker after unambiguous, straightforward answers [...] There is a nostalgia for the security in the womb of a safe sameness, and so we shut out the stranger and the alien; we look for security in those who can provide answers that must be unassailable because no one is permitted to dissent, to question."[2] While institutions may present themselves as reliable or permanent, Ecclesiastes warns that even these things err; to affix ourselves to them is like "chasing the wind."[3]

Alternatively, we might choose to rely only on ourselves. But the Book of James reminds us that this, too, is futile: "Now listen, you who say, 'Today or tomorrow we will go to this or that city, spend a year there, carry on business and make money.' Why, you do not even know what will happen tomorrow. What is your life? You are a mist that appears for a little while and then vanishes."[4] So many things are beyond our control.

God invites us to root ourselves in holy wisdom. This is how we build something good and lasting with our lives. As Psalm 127 says, "Unless the Lord builds a house, the work of the builders is wasted. Unless the Lord protects a city, guarding it with sentries will do no good."[5] God's love is a reliable foundation on which to build our lives. It carries us through life's high and low seasons.

Ecclesiastes also affirms that there is a time for the hard things in life. In God's loving presence, we can admit that our lives hold death alongside birth, tearing down alongside building, weeping alongside laughing.[6] God created seasons. Nature cycles through life and death as spring gives way to fall. We can lean into this and find strength in it rather than fight it or deny it. Ecclesiastes reminds us of God's perfect timing—"Yet God has made everything beautiful for its own time. He has planted eternity in the human heart, but even so, people cannot see the whole

[2] See Endnotes / [3] Ecclesiastes 3:16, 4:1, 4:4, NLT / [4] James 4:13-14, NIV / [5] Psalm 127:1, NLT / [6] Ecclesiastes 3:2-4, NLT

scope of God's work from beginning to end."[7] Where we see only the here and now, God sees eternity. Where we see nothing but chaos, God is still working.

As we lean into God's Word, may we reflect on the cyclical nature of life and our place within it. May we consider how rooting ourselves in God's eternal presence can transform our perspective. In every high and low, may we look to God.

Reflect

I. Reflect on a challenging time you've experienced in your life. Where was God's love during that period, and in what direction might God have been pointing you?

II. How can the wisdom of Ecclesiastes teach us patience through life's seasons, keeping in mind the broader divine plan for us?

III. When feeling lost, how can we shift our focus from temporary comforts to the enduring promises and love of God?

God of all seasons,
Help us embrace each season of life,
trusting in your perfect
timing and eternal presence to
guide us through.
Amen.

[7] Ecclesiastes 3:11, NLT

"

In God's loving presence, we can admit that our lives hold death alongside birth, tearing down alongside building, weeping along-side laughing.

”

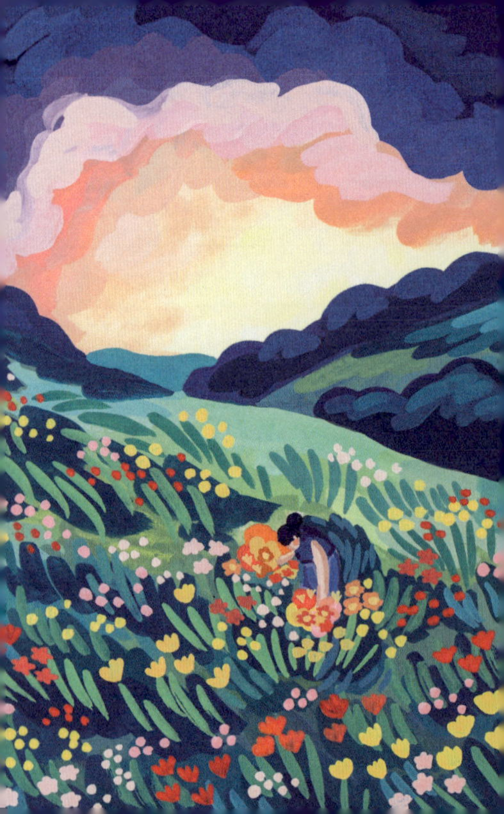

Obedience Despite Uncertainty

Synopsis

We explore how our obedience to God fosters trust, provides stability, and sets a positive, inspiring example for others in times of uncertainty.

Reading Plan

- ○ Day 1 / Deuteronomy 10-12
- ○ Day 2 / 1 Peter 1-3
- ○ Day 3 / 2 Chronicles 33-36
- ○ Day 4 / Psalms 128-130
- ○ Day 5 / Ecclesiastes 5-6
- ○ Day 6 / Haggai
- ○ Day 7 / Acts 13-14

Read—Deuteronomy 10-12

In Deuteronomy, we find the people of Israel preparing to finally enter the Promised Land. They've been through so much to get here, and are unsure of what is in store for them next. The land is still occupied and unfamiliar. Into this situation, Moses repeatedly exhorts them to obey the Lord's commands at all times and in all places. "And now, Israel, what does the Lord your God require of you? He requires only that you fear the Lord your God, and live in a way that pleases him, and love him and serve him with all your heart and soul. And you must always obey the Lord's commands and decrees that I am giving you today for your own good."[1]

We face moments of uncertainty in our lives too. Whether it's making a career change, facing health challenges, or navigating personal relationships, the future can seem daunting. Into this space of uncertainty, scripture offers several assurances. Firstly, Deuteronomy 10 reminds us

[1] Deuteronomy 10:12-13, NLT

that all of God's commands are given for our good—they are not arbitrary edicts, but intentional guides for living well and for our flourishing. Therefore, obedience, a healthy posture in all seasons, is especially helpful amidst uncertainty. When we don't know what to do, allowing God to guide our steps is the best way forward. God loves us and is trustworthy, so reliance on God is never misplaced. As the psalmist declares, "I am counting on the Lord; yes, I am counting on him. I have put my hope in his word."[2] God's faithfulness is proven and promised. No matter what we are facing, when we turn to God, we are assured we do not face it alone.[3]

Secondly, the intentional work we do to build trust in God through obedience during better times bears fruit that will carry us through seasons of struggle. This keeps us from falling back to old patterns of self-reliance when things become challenging. Regular rhythms of prayer and immersing ourselves in the wisdom of God's Word help us develop spiritual muscle memory as God's obedient children.[4] In the same way, the consistent work we do to train our hearts and minds in obedience to God will give us a strong set of habits to fall back on when we face unexpected crises.

Thirdly, scripture reminds us that consistent obedience to God makes our lives positive examples for those around us. 1 Peter 2, a letter encouraging believers to live honorably among their non-believing neighbors, states this plainly: "For this is the will of God, that by doing good you should put to silence the ignorance of foolish people. Live as people who are free, not using your freedom as a cover-up for evil, but living as servants of God."[5] Our obedience is a powerful witness to the transformative power of faith. By living respectfully and lovingly within our community, and by adhering to God's directives, we demonstrate a way of life that stands in contrast to the ways of the world.

In moments of uncertainty and challenge, may we remember these assurances from scripture and follow the instructions and guidance God has laid before us. May we strive to live in obedience, trusting that

[2] Psalm 130:5, NLT / [3] Haggai 2:4-5, NIV / [4] 1 Peter 1:14, ESV / [5] 1 Peter 2:15-16, ESV

God's plans for us are good and that divine guidance will lead us through even the most uncertain times.

Reflect

I. Think back to a time when the path of obedience to God's Word was difficult for you but you still took it. What helped strengthen you for that decision? What was the fruit of taking that path?

II. How might you build "spiritual muscle memory" that will help you to persist in obedience in difficult times? What daily practices can help you with this formation?

II. When has someone else's obedience served as an example for you? Who in your life now might be learning from your choices to obey?

Trustworthy God,
Help us to remain faithful and
obedient to your design for our lives.
May we trust that you know us—
who we are, where we've been, and
where we're going—and that you
intend only what is best for us.
Teach us that obedience is
faith and devotion in practice.
Amen.

"

Obedience, a healthy posture in all seasons, is especially helpful amidst uncertainty.

When we don't know what to do, allowing God to guide our steps is the best way forward.

”

WEEK

46

Courage in the Face of Opposition

Synopsis

Through the story of Paul and Silas in Acts 6, we explore how patience and stillness can be a radical display of courage, even in the face of opposition.

Reading Plan

- ○ Day 1 / Acts 15–16
- ○ Day 2 / 1 Peter 4–5
- ○ Day 3 / Deuteronomy 13–15
- ○ Day 4 / Ezra 1–5
- ○ Day 5 / Psalms 131–133
- ○ Day 6 / Ecclesiastes 7–8
- ○ Day 7 / Zechariah 1–7

Read— Acts 15–16

In Acts 16, a narrative of courage introduces a challenge to our expectations. We often characterize courage as something bold and brash. The word might conjure images of warriors charging into battle or adventurers facing unknown perils. Paul and Silas' story paints a contrasting picture to our perception of what it means to be courageous. Both men are unjustly arrested and harshly beaten. Locked in the prison's inner dungeon, the apostles do not attempt a grand and daring escape or rail against the guards for their mistreatment. Instead, they wait patiently, praying and praising God.[1] And, when the moment of divine deliverance comes, while they could have seized the moment and led a prisoner revolt out of the miraculously opened cells, they once again wait patiently.

[1] Acts 2:25, NLT

This posture reflects a different kind of courage, marked by stillness and gratitude. Even in their darkest hour, Paul and Silas maintain composure, patiently awaiting God's plan. Their courage is rooted in God rather than physical bravado. Their actions reflect the wisdom of Zechariah 4:6 (NIV)—"Not by might nor by power, but by my Spirit, says the Lord Almighty." It is a steadfast clinging to faith, understanding that the world moves not according to our force or will but by God alone.

Today, we often laud public figures and leaders for reacting swiftly and decisively, sometimes without forethought or patience. We celebrate men and women of action. Yet, the example set by Paul and Silas invites us to consider the strength of patience and faithfulness. The quiet act of waiting upon the Lord can yield greater results than the rush to action.

In courageously waiting upon God, Paul and Silas are not only released but profoundly influence their jailer and his family by their example. Actions rooted in patient faith rather than impulsive reactions can have far-reaching effects on others. Paul and Silas' steadfast patience and courage serve as a powerful tool for ministry, subtly drawing others closer to God. Their composed response in adversity embodies the call of 1 Peter 4:19 (NLT), "So if you are suffering in a manner that pleases God, keep on doing what is right, and trust your lives to the God who created you, for he will never fail you." When the prison cells open on his watch, the jailer's initial response is despair and impulsivity. But Paul and Silas urge him to stop and wait, ultimately saving and transforming his life.[2]

As we face the challenges of our lives, let us find inspiration in the quiet strength of Paul and Silas. Faced with the temptation of reactivity, may we reflect on the courageous nature of patience rooted in God's timing. This week, let us consider the power of a pause, the strength in stillness, and how, like a tree standing firm through the seasons, our quiet resilience can testify to faith that nurtures growth in ourselves and others. May this reflection guide us toward a deeper courage that finds its strength in faith and its voice in quiet perseverance. Amen.

 [2] Acts 16:27-34, NLT

Reflect

I. Reflect on a time when waiting and trusting in God's plan led to a better outcome than if you had acted immediately. How did that experience strengthen your faith?

II. Who in your community exemplifies patient faith, and how does their example inspire you?

III. In a society that often values quick action, how can you incorporate the biblical principle of waiting on the Lord into your daily decisions?

God of Courage,
Teach us the value of stillness.
May we trust in your timing
and embody the quiet
strength of faith.
Amen.

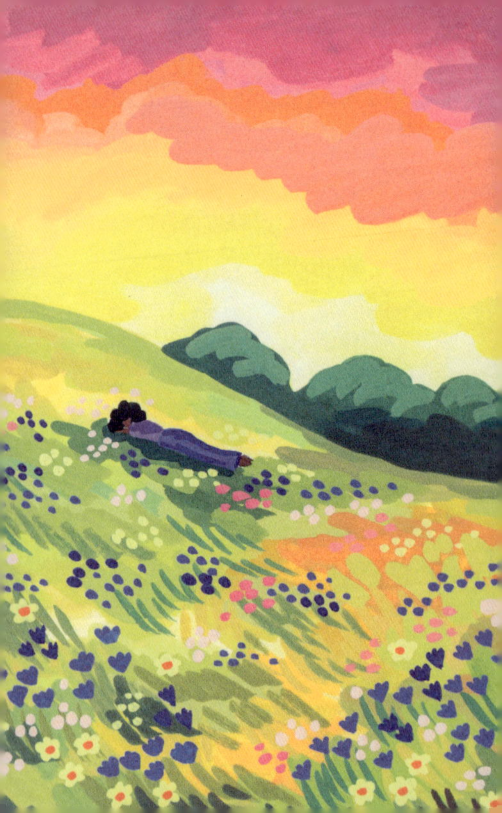

God's Enduring Love

Synopsis

Psalm 136 highlights God's unfailing, unconditional love. We reflect on the beautiful gift of divine love and how it compares to human love.

Reading Plan

- ○ Day 1 / Psalms 134–136
- ○ Day 2 / 2 Peter
- ○ Day 3 / Deuteronomy 16–19
- ○ Day 4 / Ezra 6–10
- ○ Day 5 / Ecclesiastes 9–10
- ○ Day 6 / Zechariah 8–14
- ○ Day 7 / Acts 17–18

Read—Psalms 134–136

Of all the words in our collective vocabularies, perhaps the most ubiquitous is "love." We apply the word liberally; we love our children, we love dessert, we love that song. Yet, as quickly as we declare our love for something, we often fall out of love. In stark contrast, the Bible is full of declarations of God's unfailing love. Perhaps most famously, Psalm 136 makes this very notion its repeated refrain: "His love endures forever."[1] Humans are imperfect; it stands to reason that we often fail at loving perfectly. Yet, as we experience the love of our perfect Creator, our relationships with one another are also transformed. What sets the love of God apart from earthly love?

God's love prevails through all situations, ringing out from the very beginning to the very end of all things.[2] The repeated phrase in Psalm

[1] Psalm 136:1, NLT / [2] Psalm 136:5-6, NLT

136 reminds us that God's love is with us always. Whether we are experiencing our highest highs—like Ezra and the people finally returning to Jerusalem to rebuild the Temple[3]—or our lowest lows,[4] God's love remains steadfast and unwavering. Divine love is constant and dependable. God loved each of us before we were ever born and will continue to love us after our bodies pass away.

In addition, God's love is completely unconditional, bestowed upon us no matter who we are or what we do. This is not a love we can earn, but a gift freely given. It is the fundamental spark of all creation, the impetus for God's crafting of the world, and the catalyst for the determination to save us from ourselves and bring us back into harmony with our Creator. This love is not a passive force but an active, all-encompassing pursuit that seeks to restore and redeem us, showcasing a depth and commitment that we can barely comprehend. As Zechariah 8 assures us, "All this may seem impossible to you now, a small remnant of God's people. But is it impossible for me? says the Lord of Heaven's Armies."[5] Indeed, the breadth of God's care and compassion for us is often veiled by our human perspective. 2 Peter illuminates this, reframing what we might deem slowness of God as an act of patience for our own good.[6] God's love is perfect even amidst our imperfections. God's love is total even when our understanding is partial.

As we reflect on the nature of God's love, let us consider how this divine example can transform our own expressions of love. How can we take our cues from Psalm 136, giving thanks for God's enduring love all the days of our lives? In what ways can we allow the constancy and reliability of God's love to inspire us to love others more deeply and selflessly? Let us come to this week's readings with open hearts and minds, allowing our eyes to be opened to how abundantly we are loved.

[3] Ezra 7:11-28, NLT / [4] Ecclesiastes 9:12, NIV / [5] Zechariah 8:6, NLT / [6] 2 Peter 3:8-9, NIV

Reflect

I. Think of a time when you felt loved by someone (either God or another human being). What did it feel like? How did it change you?

II. Reflect on a time when loving someone was challenging or even painful for you. How did you persevere?

III. Love is not only a feeling; it's an action. What are some ways in which you can show love actively for the people around you?

Enduring God of love,
Just as we receive your love freely,
may we learn how to give love
freely and enduringly.
In the highs and lows of
this tumultuous life,
may we hold fast to your
perfect love and express love
as constantly as you do.
Amen.

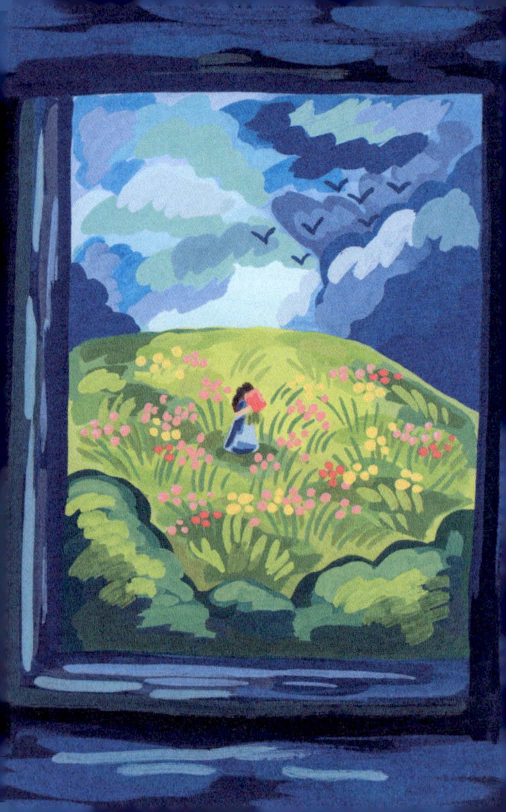

WEEK 48

The Call to Return to God

Synopsis

In Malachi, God extends an open call to return to divine grace and light. Amid temptations to go our own way, God is dependable and good, steering us back to safer harbors.

Reading Plan

- ◯ Day 1 / Malachi
- ◯ Day 2 / 1 John 1–3
- ◯ Day 3 / Deuteronomy 20–22
- ◯ Day 4 / Nehemiah 1–4
- ◯ Day 5 / Psalms 137–139
- ◯ Day 6 / Ecclesiastes 11–12
- ◯ Day 7 / Acts 19–20

Read—Malachi

One of the prophetic books of the Bible, Malachi serves as a divine call for the people of Israel to return to God. Following a period of turmoil and exile, the people have been allowed to return to Jerusalem, but they are still not living in accordance with God's ways.[1] Here then, God confronts them about their disobedience and urges them to run back to their rightful Creator. To our modern ear, some of the language used by God in Malachi (and indeed, elsewhere in scripture) may seem harsh. But while these direct rebukes may make us uncomfortable at first, they underscore God's deep desire to restore humanity to a state of intimate closeness, reflecting God's unwavering commitment to our greatest good.

Malachi emphasizes that amidst our restless wanderings, God is reliable, offering an open invitation to turn around and return. "'I am the

[1] Malachi 1:12-14, NLT

Lord, and I do not change [...] Ever since the days of your ancestors, you have scorned my decrees and failed to obey them. Now return to me, and I will return to you.'"[2] This imagery is powerful, illustrating that the door to God's grace is always open. God's pursuit of our hearts is a recurring theme throughout the Bible. Consider Psalm 139, which celebrates God's intimate knowledge of us and God's persistent presence in our lives, even when we attempt to hide. This depiction of God's omnipresence reassures us that we are never out of reach. Pastor and speaker Francis Chan states this explicitly: "No soul is too far gone for God to bring back. No heart is too hard for God to soften. No son or daughter is too lost for God to rescue."[3]

In this way, God is like a lighthouse guiding drifting ships safely to harbor. God's firm warnings are meant to steer us away from danger and toward safety, towards divine light. Even in our darkest moments, God's light shines through, urging us to return. This heartfelt pursuit is not about condemnation but about offering second chances—God is constantly working to bring us back into the fold. 1 John makes this idea explicitly clear: "This is the message we heard from Jesus and now declare to you: God is light, and there is no darkness in him at all. So we are lying if we say we have fellowship with God but go on living in spiritual darkness; we are not practicing the truth. But if we are living in the light, as God is in the light, then we have fellowship with each other."[4] We are not designed to merely feel God's light, but to live in it! Divine warnings are beacons of hope and direction in our lives, illuminating the path back to our Creator. They are a call to step away from the shadowy seas of dishonesty and selfishness and into the clarity and safety of God's radiant presence.

The call of God is constant and consistent throughout time. From the very beginning, God's desire for us has been the same: for us to live communally in perfect Shalom. When we feel lost, this reminder rings out to us, pointing us to an eternal fellowship with our loving God. These instructions are not new but are part of the timeless command to live in the light by loving one another.[5] Love is what truly makes a place to live home, and God is love.

[2] Malachi 3:6-7, NLT / [3] See Endnotes /
[4] 1 John 1:5-7, NLT / [5] 1 John 2:7-8, NLT

As we ruminate on these passages, may we recognize the areas where we have strayed and seek God's guidance to navigate back. Let us prepare our hearts to respond to the divine call, knowing that God's light will always lead us to the safe harbor of perfect love. May we find the strength to turn towards God, and receive a homecoming for the heart that is offered to us all.

Reflect

I. Reflect on Ecclesiastes 11–12's wisdom about life's uncertainties. How does this perspective help you understand the importance of returning to and relying on God's guidance?

II. What are the areas in your life where you might be drifting from God's ways? Take a moment, without judgment, to talk with God about the areas that come to mind.

III. Consider the metaphor of God as a lighthouse. What steps can you take to steer back towards living fully in God's light?

God of Grace,
I belong with you.
Forgive us for following our own ways and wandering from you.
Lead us, by your light and your love, back home.
Amen.

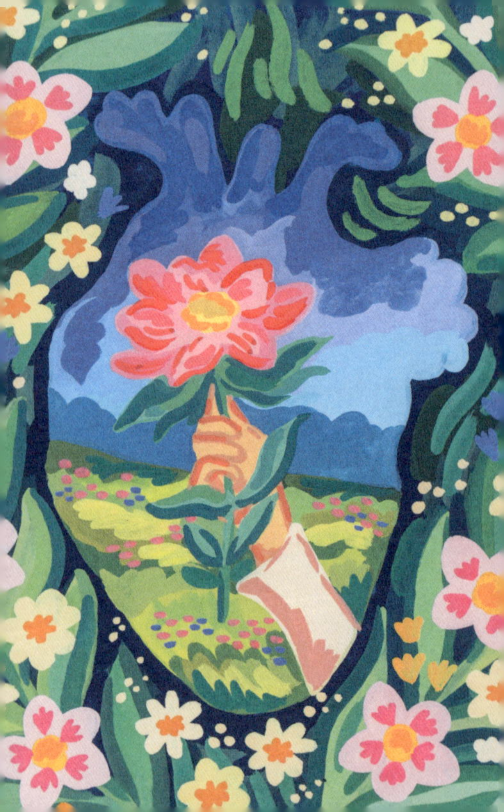

The Greatest Commandment (Love)

Synopsis

1 John 4 establishes God as love and invites us to embody this fundamental, transformative, and selfless force in all we do in our lives.

Reading Plan

- ○ Day 1 / 1 John 4–5
- ○ Day 2 / Deuteronomy 23–25
- ○ Day 3 / Nehemiah 5–9
- ○ Day 4 / Psalms 140–142
- ○ Day 5 / The Song of Songs 1–2
- ○ Day 6 / Revelation 1–6
- ○ Day 7 / Acts 21–22

Read— 1 John 4–5

1 John 4 offers an extensive exploration of the absolute "greatest commandment": love.[1] Love is a steadfast throughline of scripture, expressed and invoked countless times in both Testaments. But what sets it above all other virtues? Why is love so central, and what does it really mean to live this commandment out?

All that is good comes from God; from the pleasant beauty of nature to the melodious sounds of laughter, our Creator is the source of everything wonderful. And yet, the author of 1 John makes a key distinction: love is not just *from* God, God *is* love.[2] It is the spark that brings creation into being, the lifeblood and foundation of all other blessings, the epitome. To personify God as love opens up an entirely new revelation of what this word means. Not only does it show us who God is, but in this single word, God's very character and heart of existence is summed up. In the words of 1 John 4:16 (NIV), "Whoever lives in love lives

[1] Matthew 22:37-39, NIV / [2] 1 John 4:16, NIV

in God, and God in them." This makes love the most essential aspect of a life of faith. If we claim to follow God but do not love, we have fundamentally missed the point.[3] God and love are inextricably linked.

Love is not just a general sense of pleasantness or politeness extended to others, but a powerful and transformative force that can change lives. The Song of Songs 2:7 speaks to the mighty potential of love, cautioning us not to approach it lightly or flippantly. Showing love to one another is the most essential reflection of the divine. True love is sacrificial and selfless, mirroring the love God so freely shows us. Revelation 2 likewise affirms the centrality of love. We are told that the church of Ephesus has been, on the whole, relatively faithful. But there is still cause for rebuke from God—"Yet I hold this against you: You have forsaken the love you had at first."[4] In falling away from love, all other displays of righteousness ring false. A lack of love reflects a dismissal of the image of God present in our fellow human beings. Conversely, when we truly live out of a posture of love, we are moved to generosity, patience, kindness, gentleness, and all other signifiers of spiritual flourishing.

The truth is, we are only able to experience and express this love because God first loved us.[5] Divine love is unwavering, embracing us in our messiness and imperfections. It is sacrificial, willing to go the extra mile for someone else's well-being. Following that example, we are called to extend love to all the world, even those we find it difficult to love. We need not fear each other on account of differences and disagreements; as 1 John assures us, "There is no fear in love. But perfect love drives out fear, because fear has to do with punishment."[6] Theologian A. W. Tozer unpacks this verse powerfully: "Love casts out fear, for when we know we are loved, we are not afraid. Whoever has God's perfect love, fear is gone out of the universe for him."[7] While the specter of fear may seem a constant presence in our lives, be it in the form of stress, worry, illness, or trauma, we have the freedom to choose love. It is the stronger force that will always expel us

[3] 1 John 4:7-8, NIV / [4] Revelation 2:4, NIV /
 [5] 1 John 4:19, NIV / [6] 1 John 4:18, NIV / [7] See Endnotes

out of that uncertain darkness and into a place of pure safety. Let us open our hearts to love more deeply, recognizing its power to unite, heal, and transform our world. Let us live out this divine commandment, ensuring that love remains at the center of all our actions and relationships.

Reflect

I. What changes might occur in your daily interactions and relationships by embodying the love described in 1 John 4?

II. In what ways can you more deeply commit to expressing genuine love in your daily life?

III. Consider Revelation 2:4's warning against "forsaking the love you had at first." In what areas of your life do you need to rekindle your initial fervor and commitment to loving others?

God of Love,
You are the definition of love.
Fill us with your divine love,
that we may live fully
in its power,
extending grace and unity to all.
Amen.

“Whoever lives in love lives

in God,
and God
in them.

”

— I JOHN 4:16

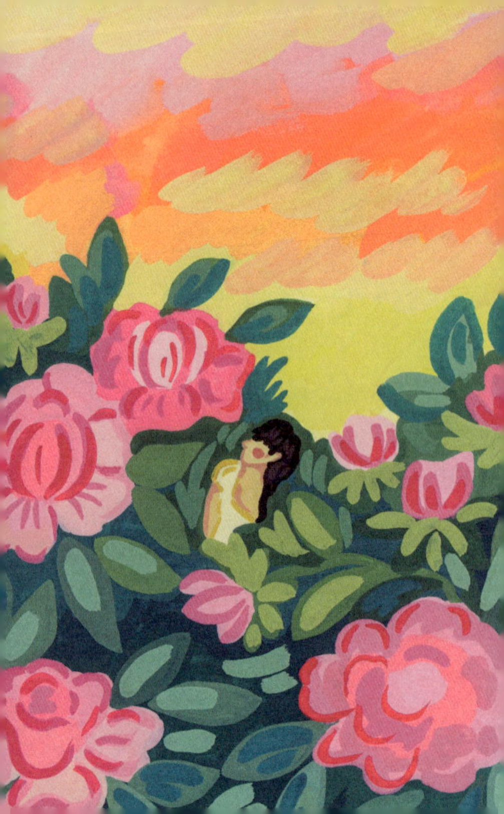

The Beauty of Intimacy

Synopsis

The Song of Songs celebrates the beauty of human intimacy and invites us to explore the ways in which it is a sacred and integral part of our faith journey.

Reading Plan

- ○ Day 1 / The Song of Songs 3–4
- ○ Day 2 / 2 John
- ○ Day 3 / Deuteronomy 26–28
- ○ Day 4 / Nehemiah 10–13
- ○ Day 5 / Psalms 143–145
- ○ Day 6 / Revelation 7–11
- ○ Day 7 / Acts 23–24

Read—The Song of Songs 3–4

As we read through the entirety of scripture, the Songs of Songs may surprise us. By its nature, it is an erotic poem, celebrating the most intimate forms of human love. Amid the histories, the genealogies, and the theological letters we find elsewhere in the Bible, it's easy to find ourselves surprised (or even shocked) when we get to this book. And yet, the Song of Songs presents us with a profound truth: human love—romantic and sexual—is holy. It boldly asserts that love and desire are divine gifts. As the young people in the poem eloquently speak of their devotion to one another, we are presented with a picture of human intimacy that is beautiful and good. "Your love delights me, my treasure, my bride. Your love is better than wine, your perfume more fragrant than spices."[1] The metaphors in these stanzas show that romantic and erotic love are not frivolous, but are pinnacles of human connection.

[1] The Song of Songs 4:10, NLT

What role do romance and eroticism play in a Christian life? Too often our world presents a fragmented view of sexuality and faith, compartmentalizing these aspects of human experience. But the Song of Songs demonstrates that, within the Bible's narrative, it is misguided to try to divorce these two areas of life. Such love is indeed a divine gift. The plentiful garden imagery in the Song points us back to Eden and the intended state of humanity. In Genesis, we see creation as God designed it to be: a couple together in a flourishing garden, nature in harmony. The Song of Songs uses similar imagery to evoke this original harmony. As theologian Phyllis Trible writes, "In many ways, then, Song of Songs is a midrash[2] on Genesis 2–3 [...] Female and male are born to mutuality and love. They are naked without shame; they are equal without duplication. They live in gardens where nature joins in celebrating their oneness."[3]

The Song of Songs shows us how the erotic, in its most pure form, is an expression of intimacy. Trible notes, "They treat each other with tenderness and respect, for they are sexual lovers, not sexual objects. They neither exploit nor escape sex; they embrace and enjoy it."[4] God intends for romantic and sexual love to be rooted in mutual respect. When we love one another well, we honor God. This mandate rings out from the dawn of creation: "Love means doing what God has commanded us, and he has commanded us to love one another, just as you heard from the beginning."[5]

Therefore, the intimacy of sex and romance should not be denigrated or feared, but instead be viewed as an expression of creation's most beautiful state. Romance, sexuality, desire, passion—these are not separate from our spiritual lives, but integral components that deepen our relationship with God and one another. In expressions of intimacy, love becomes embodied. The sacred becomes intermingled with the earthly; the anticipated becomes realized. In our love for one another, we gain a richer understanding of the depth and breadth of God's love

 [2, 3, 4] See Endnotes / [5] 2 John 1:6, NLT

for us. As we reflect on these scriptures, let us appreciate the sanctity of intimacy, recognizing it as a part of our faith journey.

Reflect

I. In what ways were you taught, implicitly or explicitly, to separate the love expressed through romance and intimacy from the love of God?

II. How can you see divine love reflected in your own experiences of sexuality and intimate relationships?

III. How can we practice respect, consent, and mutuality in ways that honor God's design for loving relationships?

Creator of Intimacy,
As we learn not to shy away from
closeness with you,
may we learn not to shy away from
intimate closeness with others.
Show us the beauty you created,
revealed through romance & sexuality,
so that we may experience the
fullness of life you intended for us.
Amen.

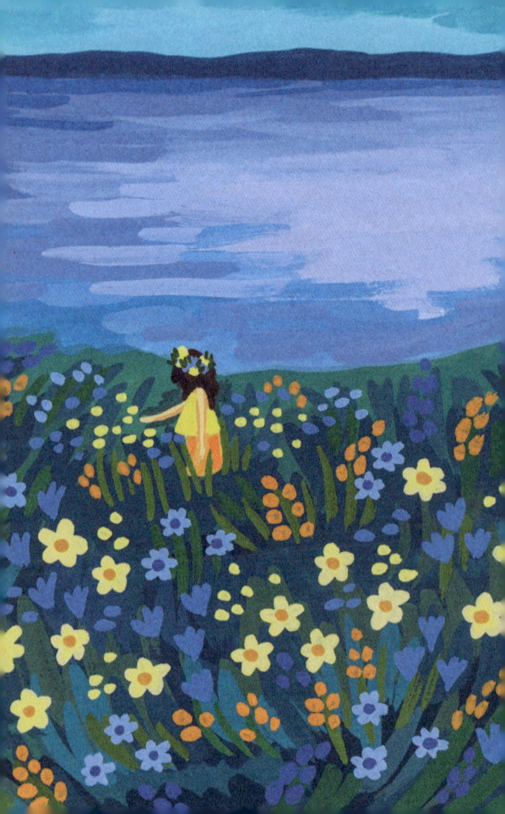

WEEK 51

The Power of Advocacy

Synopsis

In Esther's courage to stand up for justice, we are moved to follow her example in advocating for ourselves and others, trusting that God supports us in our efforts against systems of oppression.

Reading Plan

- ○ Day 1 / Esther 1–5
- ○ Day 2 / 3 John
- ○ Day 3 / Deuteronomy 29–31
- ○ Day 4 / Psalms 146–148
- ○ Day 5 / The Song of Songs 5–6
- ○ Day 6 / Revelation 12–17
- ○ Day 7 / Acts 25–26

Read—Esther 1–5

The Book of Esther tells the story of a young Jewish woman who becomes the queen of Persia and bravely advocates for her people when they are threatened with annihilation. Standing up for those she loves is an act that requires great personal risk. Still, Esther remains committed to doing what is right no matter the cost—"If I must die, I must die."[1] How can we learn from Esther's brave example? What does it mean to advocate for oneself and for others? And how does God meet us in our advocacy?

Scripture resoundingly conveys the true character of the Lord as just, compassionate, protective, merciful, and righteous. Therefore, everything that God does embodies inherently each of these qualities. As the Psalms declare, "He gives justice to the oppressed and food to the hungry.

[1] Esther 4:16, NLT

The Lord frees the prisoners. The Lord opens the eyes of the blind. The Lord lifts up those who are weighed down. The Lord loves the godly. The Lord protects the foreigners among us. He cares for the orphans and widows, but he frustrates the plans of the wicked."[2] To advocate, then, is to align ourselves with God's desires in the face of human opposition.

When we witness the forces and powers of this world attempting to dehumanize, harm, degrade, disenfranchise, and mistreat others, we are called to speak out against these injustices. In doing so, we partner with God in the significant work of ushering in justice and love. 3 John 1:11 (NIV) reminds us of our responsibility as believers: "Dear friend, do not imitate what is evil but what is good. Anyone who does what is good is from God. Anyone who does what is evil has not seen God." Advocacy is our faith made active—by responding to God's call in this way, we live into the Kingdom here and now.

Sometimes, advocating for what is right can feel daunting and perilous. Even Esther was initially hesitant to act due to the severe grave dangers she might face. In the midst of this uncertainty, her cousin offered counsel: "Mordecai sent this reply to Esther: 'Don't think for a moment that because you're in the palace you will escape when all other Jews are killed. If you keep quiet at a time like this, deliverance and relief for the Jews will arise from some other place, but you and your relatives will die. Who knows if perhaps you were made queen for just such a time as this?'"[3] We can glean several insights from this reply. First, we can be assured that God's people will be delivered by God. Second, we realize God's call to action is for all. Scripture warns against hiding behind power or privilege while leaving others to fend for themselves. Finally, we can take comfort in knowing that we are never alone; God remains with us, and challenging circumstances can be reframed as an invitation from God to partner in divine plans.

Deuteronomy 31:6 encourages us: "So be strong and courageous! Do not

 [2] Psalm 146:7-9, NLT / [3] Esther 4:13-14, NLT

be afraid and do not panic before them. For the Lord your God will personally go ahead of you. He will neither fail you nor abandon you." We are not alone, and we act with God against injustice, as individuals and in Christian community. When we reflect on scripture this week, may we find the courage to stand up for what is right, knowing that, in doing so, we walk hand in hand with God. Amen.

Reflect

I. Esther takes great risks to advocate for her community, pushing past rigid barriers and knowing she may die. Have you ever felt called by God to do something that, at the time, felt risky or out of your comfort zone? What happened?

II. Who are the oppressed, hungry, imprisoned, disabled, foreigners, orphans, and widows of our society today? How can we see their needs with eyes like those of the God of Justice?

III. How do you think the Lord may be asking you to advocate for someone in need today?

Almighty Advocate,
May you go before us and walk beside us
as we draw near to the
brokenhearted and downtrodden.
Give us the courage and boldness of Esther
to be advocates for those
who need justice and healing.
Amen.

"

So be strong & courageous! Do not be afraid and do not panic before them. For the Lord your God will personally go ahead of you. He will neither fail you nor abandon you.

”

— DEUTERONOMY 31:6

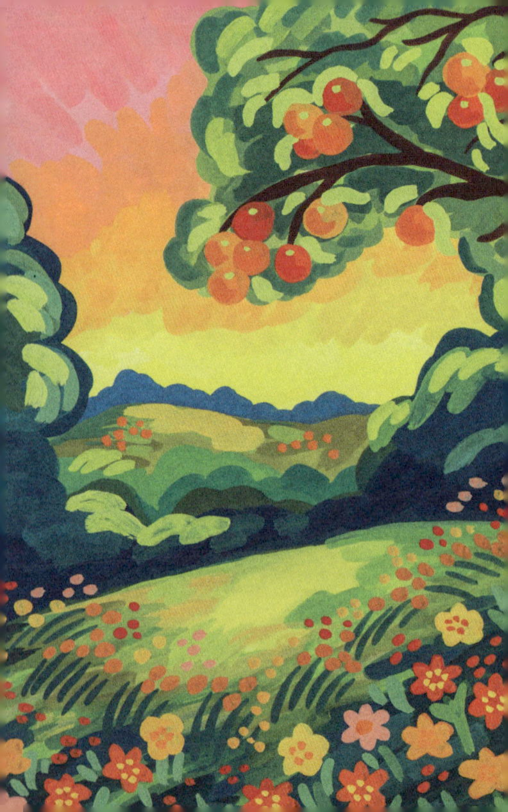

Creation Made Whole

Synopsis

We complete our journey through the scriptures together with the grand vision of Revelation 21–22—a new heaven and earth where God dwells among us, calling us to imagine and work towards the flourishing and Shalom for all of creation.

Reading Plan

- ○ Day 1 / Revelation 18–22
- ○ Day 2 / Jude
- ○ Day 3 / Deuteronomy 32–34
- ○ Day 4 / Esther 6–10
- ○ Day 5 / Psalms 149–150
- ○ Day 6 / The Song of Songs 7–8
- ○ Day 7 / Acts 27–28

Read— Revelation 18–22

In these final chapters of the Bible, we come face to face with imagery that harkens back to the very beginning in Genesis 1–2 and the Garden of Eden. Revelation 21:3-4 reads, "Look, God's home is now among his people! He will live with them, and they will be his people. God himself will be with them. He will wipe every tear from their eyes, and there will be no more death or sorrow or crying or pain. All these things are gone forever." The message is clear—God is making all things new. Once again, as in the Garden, God walks among us. Pain and sorrow are no more.

In Revelation, we witness a transformation: a new heaven and a new earth.[1] The river of life flows from God's throne, and trees of life grow, providing healing and sustenance.[2] These verses depict creation in

[1] Revelation 21:1, NLT / [2] Revelation 22:1-2, NLT

abundance—the absolute definition of Shalom. Barriers and divisions give way to freedom and togetherness. We are united with our Creator, and all things flourish. Love abounds. The automatic response of worship rings out from every corner—"Let everything that breathes sing praises to the Lord!"[3]

Biblically, we cling to this hope of flourishing, but experientially, we see that things are not as they should be. It is in this place of tension that we journey—building families, neighboring, working, and worshiping. It is in this place that we navigate systems of injustice that impact our communities; in this place we see the natural world exploited and denigrated for economic gain. In the midst of this, we ask the Spirit to help us imagine and participate in the beauty of our collective flourishing. With faith in God's good plan, we co-create beauty toward flourishing.

This is the good plan God has had from the beginning. In the words of biblical professor J. Richard Middleton, "Salvation is conceived not as God doing something completely new, but rather as redoing something, fixing or repairing what went wrong [...] This restorative work is applied as holistically and comprehensively as possible, to all things in heaven and on earth."[4] Even when we experience tension as we live our lives here and now, we catch a taste of this bounty that we read of in scripture. As we pursue mutual flourishing and care for one another and the planet, we live into the creation that is to come. The Book of Jude echoes this refrain, encouraging us to "build each other up in [our] most holy faith, pray in the power of the Holy Spirit, and await the mercy of our Lord Jesus Christ, who will bring you eternal life."[5] By supporting a reality where all can flourish, we participate in God's plan for a restored world—a place where we dwell in God's love and presence forever. This final vision in Revelation assures us that our faith and perseverance have not been in vain. Creation will be made whole; God's peace and love reign supreme.

As we reflect on the culmination of the scriptures, let us find comfort and motivation in the promise of renewal. If we place the lessons and

 [3] Psalm 150:6, NLT / [4] See Endnotes / [5] Jude 1:20-21, NLT

insights of the Bible at the center of our lives, we can imagine this new heaven and a new earth here and now. Every act of love, kindness, and worship brings us closer to the divine ideal. Let us prepare our hearts and communities for the day when God will make all things new. Amen.

Reflect

I. What images arise when considering the promise of a new creation with no more sorrow or tears? What images of pain do these replace?

II. How might we participate in the flourishing of all people today as a way of embodying this new creation?

III. Participation in this renewed view of creation extends not just to all people but to the natural world as well. How can we live into this vision in our care and stewardship of the planet?

God of Restoration,
You make all things new.
Help us pursue the flourishing of
all of creation
as we await the
fulfillment of your promises.
Amen.

"

Look, God's home is now among his people! He will live with them,

& they will be his people. God himself will be with them.

”

REVELATION 21:3

ALABASTER

BRIAN CHUNG

CHRISTINA WOO

COLLIN ELDRIDGE

ELLEN WEI

EMMA TWEITMANN

ESTHER CHOI

GABRIEL QUINTANAR

JOHN HAN

JOSH YOON

KIM HUEZO

JOYCE TAN

MINZI BAE

SAMUEL HAN

TYLER ZAK

VALERIE HUI

WILLA JIN

RACHEL CHANG

Layout Designer

RACHEL YUMI CHUNG

Artwork

CHAPTER	EDITOR
Relationship Between God & Humanity	Emma Tweitmann
Divine Guidance & Provision	Sabrina Dawson
New Beginnings	Bethany Fox
God's Unbreakable Promises	Katie McEachern
Trust in God's Unfathomable Nature	Tamar Peterson
Seeking Inner Righteousness	Sandra Van Opstal
God Delivers Us	Mattea Gernentz
Heeding God's Calling	Bethany Fox
Wrestling with Faith & Judgment	Alexis Ragan
Complexity of Relationships	Tamar Peterson
Steadfast Faith in Times of Sorrow	Sabrina Dawson
Anticipating a Better Future	Tamisha Tyler
Learning from Past Lessons	Bethany Fox
God Values the Weak & Vulnerable	Bethany Fox
The Beauty of Serving Others	Sabrina Dawson
God is Our Refuge	Mary Taylor
God is Mighty	Bethany Fox
Hope & Patient Expectation	Roslyn Hernandez
God's Vision & Plans	Mattea Gernentz
Living Generously	Tamar Peterson
God's Transformative Grace	Adrian Patenaude
Pursuing Wisdom	Bethany Fox
Extending Hospitality	Bethany Fox
Unity through Inclusion	Tamisha Tyler
Repairing Relationships	Roslyn Hernandez
Finding God in Quietness	Sabrina Dawson

CHAPTER	EDITOR
The Nature of God's Kingdom	Mary Taylor
Freedom & Reconciliation in Christ	Alexis Ragan
Divine Justice in an Unjust World	Emma Tweitmann
Community of Believers	Jackie Aviles
Flourishing in God's Presence	Elizabeth Cooledge Jenkins
Strength & Perseverance	Jackie Aviles
The Joy of Worship	Mattea Gernentz
The Gift of Forgiveness	Alexis Ragan
Divine Callings	Elizabeth Cooledge Jenkins
The Holy Spirit is Our Advocate	Jessica Galvan
Leading Well	Elizabeth Cooledge Jenkins
Work of the Cross	Emma Tweitmann
The Greatness of God	Mary Taylor
Compassion & Second Chances	Mary Taylor
Jesus is Our Redeemer	Mary Taylor
Sharing Our Faith	Bethany Fox
Living Out Our Faith	Emma Tweitmann
Embracing Life's Seasons	Elizabeth Cooledge Jenkins
Obedience Despite Uncertainty	Bethany Fox
Courage in the Face of Opposition	Betsy Sunny
God's Enduring Love	Adrian Patenaude
The Call to Return to God	Alexis Ragan
The Greatest Commandment (Love)	Alexis Ragan
The Beauty of Intimacy	Tamar Peterson
The Power of Advocacy	Mattea Gernentz
Creation Made Whole	Sandra Van Opstal

Endnotes

Divine Guidance & Provision

- [2] Matthew 4:13-16, NIV. Another example of this continual promise is John the Baptist, himself a fulfillment of Isaiah's prophecy (Isaiah 40:3). John comes to prepare the way for Jesus, illuminating the path that Jesus will invite us to walk alongside him.

God's Unbreakable Promises

- [2] Genesis 15:9-18 presents a picture of a traditional covenant ceremony, with animal offerings and passed torches to symbolize the sealing of the agreement. Notice that only something representing God passes through the meat, nothing representing Abram. This suggests a one-sided covenant, with only one party bound to follow through.

God Delivers Us

- [4] Philip Yancey, *What Good Is God? On the Road with Stories of Grace* (London: Hodder & Stoughton, 2012).

Heeding God's Calling

- [3] Joseph Campbell, *The Hero's Journey: Joseph Campbell on His Life and Work* (United States: Joseph Campbell Foundation, 2020).

Wrestling with Faith & Judgment

- [3] Jennifer Slattery, "Wrestling with God When Something in the Bible Bothers You," *Jennifer Slattery Lives Out Loud* (blog), March 31, 2022, https://jenniferslatterylivesoutloud.com/tag/wrestling-with-god/

Complexity of Relationships

- [1] Henri J.M. Nouwen. Exploration of Themes on Grace, Reconciliation, and Healing. *The Wounded Healer, The Return of the Prodigal Son, Life of the Beloved.* Various publishers, Various publication years.
- [2] See also the story of Judah and Tamar in Genesis 38 which showcases an unconventional family conflict. When Judah fails to uphold his responsibilities to his daughter-in-law, Tamar seeks justice in an

unexpected way, at great personal risk because her situation is that dire. While jarring to us today, the result is accountability from Judah and restoration for Tamar.

- [3] Vitally, embracing the complexity of relationships does not mean enduring abuse with no accountability. Healthy boundaries are important and justified when safety and well-being are threatened. Forgiveness can be extended without maintaining proximity and intimacy. Sometimes distance is a prerequisite to healing.

Steadfast Faith in Times of Sorrow

- [2] Barbara Brown Taylor, *Learning to Walk in the Dark* (New York: HarperCollins, 2014).

God Values the Weak & Vulnerable

- [1] Charles Dickens, *A Christmas Carol* (Oxford University: Bradbury & Evans, 1858), 9.

- [3] Jesus' reference to "dogs" in this passage may strike us as disturbing; it seems dismissive and insulting. However, the form of the word used by Jesus in the original text is more diminutive, implying "household pets" rather than street scavengers. Such dogs are part of the family but are fed afterward, drawing on the scriptural distinction between the Gentiles and the Jews as God's special people. The woman's clever and humble response embraces the metaphor, showing her faith and understanding. Jesus honors her persistence and faith, showcasing the inclusivity of God's grace beyond cultural boundaries.

Living Generously

- [3] Our place in this community is not only that of a giver. And, indeed, sometimes asking for and accepting help can be even more challenging. Being vulnerable enough to ask for help actually strengthens the bonds of community. Healthy human relationships are reciprocal. Embodying generosity can also mean allowing others to meet us in our need.

God's Transformative Grace

- [1] 2 Samuel 11–12, NLT. Beyond this egregious instance, scripture tells us that David was consistently tempted to abuse his power throughout his rule. It is humbling to see how God continued to lovingly challenge him in this lifelong tendency, even at the very end of his life.

Unity Through Inclusion

- [2] As displayed in Leviticus 1–3. Here specific directives for honoring God and making amends are equalizing; the means of offering glorifying sacrifices are the same for all of God's people.

Repairing Relationships

- [4] Notably, inflicting hurt is not reserved only for individuals. Our institutions and communities miss the mark as well. We know too well the pain that has been caused by families, by governments, and even (tragically) by churches. In these circumstances, the difficult work of repair and reconciliation can be even more complex.
- [5] Martin Luther King, "'Remaining Awake Through a Great Revolution,'" *Commencement Address for Oberlin College* (address presented at the Oberlin College Commencement, Oberlin: Ohio, June 1965).

Finding God in Quietness

- [3] Henri J. M. Nouwen, *Out of Solitude: Three Meditations on the Christian Life* (Notre Dame, Ind: Ave Maria Press, 2004), 61.

Freedom and Reconciliation in Christ

- [2] Elisabeth Elliot, *Let Me Be A Woman* (Carol Stream, Ill: Tyndale House Publishers, Inc, 2013).

Divine Justice in an Unjust World

- [3] Jessica Nicholas, *God Loves Justice: A User-Friendly Guide to Biblical Justice and Righteousness* (Los Angeles, CA: S & E Educational Press, 2017).

Community of Believers

- [2] PBSNewsHour, *'My Humanity Is Caught up in Yours': How Desmond*

Tutu Dedicated His Life to Greater Good, broadcast, https://www.youtube.com/watch?v=w7V1h4soUk.

- [3] Coretta Scott King and Barbara A. Reynolds, *My Life, My Love, My Legacy* (New York: Henry Holt and Company, 2017).

Flourishing in God's Presence

- [3] Lisa Sharon Harper, *Fortune: How Race Broke My Family and the World—and How to Repair It All* (Ada: Brazos Press 2022), 140.

The Gift of Forgiveness

- [3] In the shadows of perfectionism, extending grace to ourselves for mistakes can be especially difficult. Self-condemnation is the heaviest weight our hearts can bear, and holding onto what we have done wrong can hinder our embrace of the gift of forgiveness. God invites us to let go and look forward, allowing forgiveness to heal us.

Leading Well

- [4] Greg Boyle, *Tattoos On The Heart: The Power of Boundless Compassion* (Winnipeg: Manitoba Education and Advanced Learning, Alternate Formats Library, 2014), 188.

- [5] Dr. Brenda Salter McNeil, *Becoming Brave: Finding the Courage to Pursue Racial Justice Now* (Ada: Brazos Press, 2020), 179.

Compassion & Second Chances

- [3] C.S. Lewis, *The Weight of Glory* (New York: Simon & Schuster, 1996), 135-136.

Sharing Our Faith

- [4] Daniel Thambyrajah Niles, *That They May Have Life* (London: Lutterworth Press, 1954).

- [5] Another example of this is the woman of noble character in Proverbs 31, who shares her faith through both her words and her actions.

Embracing Life's Seasons

- [2] Desmond Tutu, *God Is Not a Christian: And Other Provocations* (New York: HarperOne, 2011), 4.

The Call to Return to God

- [3] Francis Chan, "No Soul Is Too Far Gone," web log, *desiring*God, November 2018, https://www.desiringgod.org/articles/no-soul-is-too-far-gone.

The Greatest Commandment (Love)

- [7] A. W. Tozer, *The Attributes of God: A Journey into the Father's Heart* (Camp Hill, Pa: Wing Spread Publications, 2007).

The Beauty of Intimacy

- [2] "Midrash" is a Jewish term for interpreting and understanding scripture. The practice of midrash is a means of exploring and making sense of contemporary questions in the context of an ancient and unchanging text.
- [3] Phyllis Trible, "Depatriarchalizing in Biblical Interpretation," *Journal of the American Academy of Religion XLI, no. 1* (1973): 47, https://doi.org/10.1093/jaarel/xli.1.30.
- [4] Trible, 46.

Creation Made Whole

- [4] J. Richard Middleton, *A New Heaven and a New Earth: Reclaiming Biblical Eschatology* (Grand Rapids, MI: Baker Academic, a division of Baker Publishing Group, 2014), 163.

Published in Los Angeles by Alabaster Creative Inc.

FSC
www.fsc.org
MIX
Paper | Supporting responsible forestry
FSC® C013123

Printed in Italy by
Graphicom S.r.l.

Contact:
hello@alabasterco.com
www.alabasterco.com

Alabaster Co explores the intersection of creativity, beauty, and faith. Founded in 2016.

Based in Los Angeles.

CONTINUE THE CONVERSATION

www.alabasterco.com